BATTLES OF DESTINY

LECTOR HOUSE PUBLIC DOMAIN WORKS

This book is a result of an effort made by Lector House towards making a contribution to the preservation and repair of original classic literature. The original text is in the public domain in the United States of America, and possibly other countries depending upon their specific copyright laws.

In an attempt to preserve, improve and recreate the original content, certain conventional norms with regard to typographical mistakes, hyphenations, punctuations and/or other related subject matters, have been corrected upon our consideration. However, few such imperfections might not have been rectified as they were inherited and preserved from the original content to maintain the authenticity and construct, relevant to the work. The work might contain a few prior copyright references as well as page references which have been retained, wherever considered relevant to the part of the construct. We believe that this work holds historical, cultural and/or intellectual importance in the literary works community, therefore despite the oddities, we accounted the work for print as a part of our continuing effort towards preservation of literary work and our contribution towards the development of the society as a whole, driven by our beliefs.

We are grateful to our readers for putting their faith in us and accepting our imperfections with regard to preservation of the historical content. We shall strive hard to meet up to the expectations to improve further to provide an enriching reading experience.

Though, we conduct extensive research in ascertaining the status of copyright before redeveloping a version of the content, in rare cases, a classic work might be incorrectly marked as not-in-copyright. In such cases, if you are the copyright holder, then kindly contact us or write to us, and we shall get back to you with an immediate course of action.

HAPPY READING!

BATTLES OF DESTINY

M. FIDES SHEPPERSON (ISABEL SHEPPERSON)

ISBN: 978-93-90294-70-1

Published: 1914

© 2020
LECTOR HOUSE LLP

LECTOR HOUSE LLP
E-MAIL: lectorpublishing@gmail.com

BATTLES OF DESTINY

BY

SISTER M. FIDES SHEPPERSON, M. A.
AUTHOR OF
"HARP OF MILAN," "CLOISTER CHORDS," Etc.

1914

CONTENTS

Chapter	Page
INTRODUCTION	vi
I. MARATHON	1
II. ARBELA	5
III. ZAMA	13
IV. TEUTOBERGER WALD	17
V. ADRIANOPLE	22
VI. CHALONS	28
VII. TOURS	32
VIII. HASTINGS-SENLAC	37
IX. ORLEANS	48
X. LEPANTO	55
XI. THE INVINCIBLE ARMADA	62
XII. NASEBY	69
XIII. BLENHEIM	79
XIV. PULTOWA	83
XV. SARATOGA	87
XVI. VALMY	90
XVII. WATERLOO	93

INTRODUCTION

This little volume will prove of interest to the general reader and of inestimable value to the student or teacher of history. It contains graphic descriptions of the seventeen great struggles of the historic past—Marathon, Arbela, Zama, Teutobergerwald, Adrianople, Chalons, Tours, Senlac-Hastings, Orleans, Lepanto, Spanish Armada, Naseby, Blenheim, Pultowa, Saratoga, Valmy, and Waterloo. Dates, figures, facts, estimates and reflections are presented in attractive form; and the net results of long research labor are given in a nutshell.

Those terrific conflicts of the past seem strangely fascinating when looked at in their crucial throes ere yet they are stamped with the die of destiny. The thoughtful mind asks, "Would our world of today be just what it is if all or if any one of these battles had borne results the reverse of what they did bear?"

CHAPTER I.
MARATHON

As in the order of time, so likewise in the order of importance, Marathon stands first among the Battles of Destiny. Without Marathon there would have been no Thermopylæ, Salamis, Platæa, Mycale; no Attic supremacy; no Age of Pericles: and would the world be just what it is today if these things had not been? Would Attica as a Persian satrapy ever have become Athens of the Acropolis crowned with the Propylaea-Erectheum-Parthenon: Athens bright star-night of the past glittering with deathless names?

Egypt, Assyria, Babylonia, Persia had risen and set; Rome subsequently rose and fell; France, Italy, Spain, England, Germany, and our own infantine experimental Republic of the West are advancing fatefully in the old circle: yet not one of these may boast as many eminent men, stars of first magnitude, glorious constellations—as little Greece might boast, that brief bright star-night of the past thick-studded with immortal names.

CALLIMACHUS, WAR RULER.

Of the ten commanders of the ten Athenian tribes who assembled on the heights overlooking the plain of Marathon, five voted against battle with the invading Persians, five in favor of battle. Callimachus the War Ruler, influenced by the enthusiastic eloquence of Miltiades, gave the casting vote in favor of battle. On this so seeming slight chance hung Marathon.

Humanly speaking, it was madness for that little handful of Greeks to rush down upon the countless Persian hosts. The Persians themselves could not believe their own eyes when they saw the Greeks running to battle; and half-heartedly, perhaps even jestingly, they prepared for a brief skirmish with madmen.

The Medes and Persians were at that time deemed invincible. Babylonia, Assyria, Asia Minor, the isles of the Ægean, the African Coast, the Euxine, Thrace, Macedonia had successively fallen before the soldiers of the Great King. The Ægean was a Persian Lake; from east, from south, from north approached the awful power of imperial Persia, ready irresistibly to absorb little Greece, to punish and obliterate Athens. Already the Eretrians, who together with the Athenians had aided in the Ionian revolt, were overtaken by the dread vengeance of Darius: their city had fallen and more than a thousand Eretrians were left bound on the island Egilia awaiting the return of the victorious Persian fleet from Marathon. Then together with the captive Athenians, the Eretrians were to be taken to Susa there to await the pleasure of the Great King, whose wrath had been new-kindled day by day with memories of burning Sardis by a court attendant whose sole duty was to repeat to Darius at each meal, "Sire, remember the Athenians." Sardis would then be fearfully avenged.

Sardis was, indeed, avenged but not by Marathon. There is a justice exact even to the weight of a hair in all things of life; seen or unseen, known or unknown, acknowledged or unacknowledged, it is ever at work silently, forcefully, fatefully. Athens burns Sardis and desecrates the temples of the Persian gods; and some years later the Persians sack and devastate Athens, razing her temples to the ground leaving her site in smoking ruins.

> "Behold there are Watchers over you, worthy Recorders, knowing what you do: and whosoever shall have wrought an ant's weight of good shall behold it; and whosoever shall have wrought an ant's weight of evil shall behold it." —*Koran.*

History tells us that after the battle of Marathon, six thousand four hundred Persians lay dead upon the battlefield and only one hundred and ninety-two Athenians. This seems incredible, yet it is equally incredible that the Greeks won. Ten thousand Athenians and one thousand Platæans had fought against one hundred thousand soldiers of the Great King, and—won. There was something wrong with that motley army of the Great King; some subtly retributive force was at work, some balancing Justice.

MILTIADES.

Doubtless to Miltiades more than to any other man Athens and the world owes Marathon. It was his overpowering eloquence that weighed heavily in the balance against the honest fears of those who dreaded the encounter with Persia's hitherto invincible warriors; the well founded fears of those who were secretly in sympathy with Hippias and hoped that a battle might be averted: and the prudent fears of those who dreaded defeat and the vengeance of the Great King and thought it wiser to wait until the promised help should come from Sparta. One man's eloquent fearlessness outweighed all those fearful considerations and precipitated the mad descent from the hill, the onslaught, the unequal fight, the wonder-victory.

Yet had Miltiades rested after the momentous battle all might have been lost. For the sullen Persian fleet hastening from Marathon had turned its course towards undefended Athens. And so that very night, even with the departure of the last Persian ship from the shore, Miltiades led his battle torn veterans a distance of about twenty-two miles to Phalerum, the port nearest to Athens. And early the next morning when, indeed, true to Miltiades' fears, the Persian fleet appeared off the coast of Phalerum, the men of Marathon stood awaiting their landing. They did not land.

Hippias, deposed tyrant of Athens, and guide and leader of the Persians was killed at Marathon. Callimachus, the polemarch, was killed, not in the battle proper, but on the shore as the defeated forces were confusedly seeking safety in escape to their ships, and the Greeks, following them even to the water's edge, kept up the slaughter.

Surely Miltiades remained ever after the best beloved hero of Athens, and his years passed on amid ever vernal honors down the easy ways of old age, and the end was in peace!

But, alas! history tells us that Miltiades fell into disgrace, was banished from Athens, and a few years after Marathon, died of his wounds in prison.

Too bad that every crest-wave of human achievement hastily tumbles to a depression correspondingly low as the swell was high. Scipio, conqueror at Zama, triumph-crowned, and honored with the appellation *Africanus*, was, on that same day one year later on trial for his life. What a tumult of conflicting feelings must have raged in his heart when, disdaining to reply to the accusations made against him, Scipio said, turning to the fickle populace, "I would remind the men of Rome that this day one year ago I won the battle of Zama." And then the tide turned in his favor and the young-world children wept because of their ingratitude, and clamorously acquitted Scipio. But depressive doubt succeeded crest confidence and Scipio went into exile. *Ingrata Patria!* (Ungrateful Native Land!) Scipio exclaimed, as death drew near and his tired eyes turned longingly towards Rome.

Coriolanus, Roman exile, torn to pieces by the Volscians; Hannibal, lone boast of Carthage, hater of Rome; Themistocles, hero of Salamis; Aristides the Just; Socrates; Miltiades are among the tragic figures on the historic stage whose dying heart-throbs may have reproachfully re-echoed *Ingrata Patria*.

ALL THE GLORY THAT WAS GREECE.

From Marathon (490 B. C.) clarion of the birth of Athens, to Ægospotami (405 B. C.) her knell of death, momentous history was made.

Ægospotami knelled the fall of Athens; Leuctra, of Sparta; Mantinea, of Epaminondas-Thebes; and Chæronea, of all Hellas; but not all of Athens died at Ægospotami. Pericles, Aspasia, Phidias, Ictinus, Socrates, Plato, Aristotle, Æschylus, Sophocles, Euripides, Aristophanes, Herodotus, Thucydides, Xenophon—have not died; they are effective forces in the world today.

Spartan military excellence, Spartan hardihood and endurance is a bubble that burst; it is no more: but Attic excellence of intellect endures imperishably—with Platonic wonder as freshly fair in college halls today as in the Academia and Lyceum of the old Athenian day. Mind is the only Conqueror.

Blue sky of Athens, white cliff Acropolis,—so unchanging amid change, so laughing fair among the ruins of the glory that was Greece!

Nature's ever young irreverence towards the wreck of time is invigorating. It calls to the heart of man in language the heart understands, *What's Time*!

"Men said, 'But time escapes
Live now or never.'
"He said, 'What's time! Leave Now for dogs and apes—
Man has Forever.'"

—Browning.

SPARTA.

The manner in which the news of the defeat of the Athenians at Ægospotami affected Athens is in striking contrast with the manner in which Sparta received word of the disastrous Spartan defeat at Leuctra. When report of the naval disaster reached the Piræus, it was quickly communicated to the thronging crowds within the Long Walls, and thence to the heart of the city. Consternation prevailed and all Athens mourned. "That night," says Xenophon, "no one in Athens slept."

The news of the defeat at Leuctra reached Sparta in the midst of a festive celebration. The magistrates heard of the defeat, and the death of their king, with countenances unmoved; they gave orders that the festival be uninterrupted; and they urged all who had lost relatives and friends in the battle of Leuctra to appear at the festivities in particularly gay attire and with smiling faces, while those whose relatives were among the survivors were ordered to put on mourning.

The spirit of Lycurgus, of Draco, and of Leonidas seems to have fused and chilled into the Laws of Sparta. No surrender; conquer or die; return with your shield or upon it; wounds all in front and faces grimly fierce even in death—such was the spirit of Sparta.

Whatever may be our admiration for the Spartan qualities in general, there can be but lament that they found expression in the Peloponnesian War. This fratricidal strife brought ruin to Hellas. Marathon, Thermopylæ, Salamis, Platæa, Mycale were all undone by Syracuse and Ægospotami. Chæronea was made possible and the passing of the scepter of empire from Greece to Macedonia, from leaderless Hellas to Alexander the Great.

CHAPTER II.
ARBELA

The life of Alexander the Great is of perennial interest, for it holds in epitome the life of the world when the world was young. Plutarch tells with quaint truthfulness what cannot now be told without a smile of wondering incredulity.

Alexander spent the night before the battle of Arbela in consultation with the diviner Aristander, and in sacrificing to the god Fear. What does that mean? The conqueror of the world would placate Fear; would render it favorable to him, adverse to the enemy. Terror, recoil from death, panic-madness of a multitude of men, rout, ruin—from *that* deliver my army, O great god Fear; but let it come upon my enemy. Thus prayed Alexander as his gaze rested upon the moving plain gleaming with a million torch-lights where Darius, prepared for a night attack, was reviewing his forces. And well might Alexander so pray. Fear that blanches the lips and freezes the blood in the heart, contagious Terror Irresistible, dread recoil from butchering death—these were, indeed, effects of causes proportionately terrible. A million men were in the enemy's ranks, three hundred chariots armed with scythes; rivers were in the rear, and beyond a hostile country.

"Alexander," says Napoleon, "deserves the glory which he has enjoyed for so many centuries and among all nations; but what if he had been beaten at Arbela, having the Euphrates, the Tigris, and the deserts in his rear, without any strong places of refuge, nine hundred leagues from Macedonia!"

After the sacrifice to the god Fear, as Plutarch gravely assures us, Alexander seemed jubilant in spirit, and returning to his tent, made ready to take his rest. Parmenio, his oldest and ablest general, sought him there and suggested that a night attack be made, urging that their army would grow faint at heart could they see as in broad daylight the countless hosts arrayed against them. In conclusion Parmenio respectfully said, "And if I were Alexander I would attack the Persians tonight."

To this Alexander ironically replied "And so would I if I were Parmenio." On further remonstrance being made Alexander curtly replied, "I will not steal a victory." At this Parmenio withdrew and Alexander lay down to rest.

A profound and most refreshing sleep came to Alexander. Morning dawned and it seemed proper to rouse the men to breakfast and to preparation for battle, but Alexander still slept. In the words of Plutarch: "But at last, time not giving them leave to wait any longer, Parmenio went to his bedside and called him twice or thrice by his name, till he waked him, and then asked how it was possible, when he was to fight the most important battle of all, he could sleep so soundly as if he were already victorious. 'And are we not so, indeed,' replied Alexander smiling, 'since we are at last relieved from the trouble of wandering in pursuit of Darius thro' a wide and wasted country, hoping in vain, that he would fight us?' And not only before the battle, but in the height of the danger, he showed himself great, and manifested the self-possession of a just foresight and confidence."

Alexander's full front battle line was not so long as Darius' center. And this so seeming fatal arrangement yet turned out to be most favorable for Alexander. For instead of attacking the Persian center where Darius commanded in person and where the ground in front had been smoothed and prepared for the rush of the three hundred scythe-chariots, Alexander attacked vigorously the left wing, driving them in front of and towards the center. The onslaught of the Macedonian phalanx was irresistible and the Persian army, dominated by the god Fear, was in panic rout before Darius could get his unwieldy forces full into action or send forth the chariots upon which he so much relied.

Alexander pursued the fleeing enemy until urged back by messengers from Parmenio saying his wing was surrounded by the Persians. Alexander reluctantly returned and full victory for the Macedonian army was soon proclaimed upon the field.

Darius, seeing that all was lost and that his chariot, wedged in among dead bodies high as the shoulders of the horses, was unable either to advance or to turn back, hastily leaped from his seat and seizing a riderless mare, he galloped as best he could over the bodies of the dying and the dead and thus escaped from the battlefield.

The break in the friendship between Alexander and his ablest general, Parmenio, began with the battle of Arbela. Was there jealousy, cruel as the grave, in the heart of the older man as he saw success after success crown the brow of the young commander? Granicus, Issus, Arbela—Europe, Asia, Africa, the world—had gone down successively under the Conqueror. Jealously is incipient hate.

> "He who ascends to mountain heights will find
> The loftiest peaks most wrapped in clouds and snow;
> He who would conquer or subdue mankind,
> Must look down on the hate of those below."
>
> —*Byron.*

HUMAN, TOO HUMAN.

All that the literatures of the world hold treasured in amber; all that life, the primal fount of literature, holds as its human heritage—find fitting application to Alexander the Great. The color scale—from white thro' tints to standard, and from standard thro' shades to black—of every emotion and passion of the heart of man is fixed fadelessly upon the name and fame of Alexander.

Yet how human and dearly human it all is! We understand it today even as Callisthenes understood it, and as the age B. C. and the early age and the middle age understood it. We haven't advanced even yet very far from the primitive. The heart that in drunken rage slew Clitus his friend, and then mourned his deed inconsolable in his tent for three days—is easily cognizable today.

That quarrel between Alexander and his tried and true Macedonians, with its subsequent reconciliation, has in it a ring of the old young-world. For when Alexander returned to Susa with his worn out troops, he at once sought out the thirty thousand boys whom he had left there in training. Great was his delight at the progress they had made in his absence; at their military bearing, their ability to ride and hurl the javelin, and to perform other adroit manœuvres. Alexander then thought to reorganize his army and send home all the Macedonians who were in any way disabled, or who, when urged to cross over the Ganges, had begged to be taken back to their wives and children. But the sturdy veterans were sorely offended at this proposal, and breaking out into a rage, declared that they had been most unjustly dealt with, and that every Macedonian would at once abandon the army, and that, perhaps, with his pretty boys he might be able to keep the world which their good swords had won for him. To this Alexander responded in deep wrath that it should be as they said. He at once dismissed from his service all the Macedonians and filled their places with Persians.

Now when the Macedonians saw that it was done even as they had said, the scales of jealous anger dropped from their eyes and they were deeply repentant. So laying aside their arms, and dressed only in short undergarments they sought suppliantly the tent of Alexander. But it opened not to their importunities. For three days they stayed there neither eating nor drinking, but sorely longing for the light of the countenance of Alexander, for every man loved him. And at last the tent door opened and Alexander came forth, and going affectionately among them he sat down and wept; and they wept.

Then Alexander, thinking it wiser that the maimed should embark in the waiting vessels, spoke to them most kindly, praising their valor and declaring that their deeds should be known throughout the world: saying also that he would write concerning them to his mother Olympias and to the Governor of Macedonia, giving orders that the first seats in the theatres should be reserved for them and that they should therein be crowned with chaplets of flowers. Moreover every soldier's pay should continue to him, and the pay due to the fallen should be regularly sent to their wives and children. And thus was reconciliation between Alexander and his Macedonians happily effected.

How childish it all is—that jealous hate and the hasty reaction; the humiliating importunities of barbaric love; the Conqueror conquered and—in tears; the generous re-fusion of the old warm feelings; the magnanimity of the Great; the joyous departure of the honored veterans, their sitting in the seats of honor crowned with a chaplet of flowers: childish? well, yes, but we older children can understand and even dimly—remember.

A DEITY.

Did Alexander believe himself descended from Jupiter Ammon? No. On one occasion being wounded he said "This, my friends, is real blood flowing not Ichor,"

"Such as immortal gods are wont to shed."

Yet if the reply of the gymnosophist be admitted as true, Alexander was not a mortal. The Gymnosophists, or wise men of India, were entertained at the court of Alexander, and among the questions proposed to them by the young lord of the world was, how a man might become a god: to this the sage replied "By doing that which was impossible for men to do." The deeds done by Alexander in his brief thirty-two years seem beyond the merely human: and it is certain that he was honored as a deity in the latter years of his life. He had his friend and biographer, Callisthenes, tortured and put to death because he had derisively laughed while the servile court prostrated before the "present Deity", and had refused to follow their example.

"Man, vain man dressed in a little brief authority does cut such capers before high heaven as make the angels mourn." The awful punishments inflicted upon Thebes, Tyre, Gaza; the maniacal madness that satiated itself in the life-blood of Clitus—a warrior, comrade, and friend, a soldier who at Granicus had thrust his own body between Alexander and the down-plunging slaughtering sword and so receiving in his own flesh the blow, had saved the life of the man who should later slay him; the deadly ingratitude which could forget the lifelong services of Parmenio, his father's ablest general, his own boyhood's adviser, admirer, and friend, and, in a fit of jealous rage, condemn to death Philotas, son of Parmenio, and Parmenio; the hate-exultation which, triumphant at last, had the feet of Batis, late satrap of Gaza and a bravely fallen foe, bored thro' and thereby tied to his chariot; then Alexander, descendant of Achilles, drove three times thro' the streets of Gaza, dragging his living victim—naked, torn, bleeding, broken, dying—thro' the town in which so late he has reigned as Persian satrap: surely at capers such as these well might the angels mourn.

Yet these atrocities are well nigh balanced by acts of heroism, repentant generosity, benignity, magnanimity: and it is an open question whether any other of the race of mortals, having the world of his time absolutely in his own hands, would have acted as wisely as Alexander.

The eunuch escaping from the Macedonian camp and bearing to Darius the news of his wife Statira's death, extolled the forbearance and chivalrous courtesy of Alexander toward the Persian captives and admiringly cried out "Alexander is as gentle after victory as he is terrible on the field." And Darius, so late King of Persia, tallest and handsomest man of his time, husband of Statira, most bewitchingly beautiful woman of Asia; but now alas! an uncrowned king, loser of Arbela, a fugitive, bereft of sons, daughters, wife—nevertheless on hearing of Alexander's generous conduct towards the royal captives exclaimed in tears, "Ye gods of my family, and of my kingdom, if it be possible, I beseech you to restore the declining affairs of Persia, that I may leave them in as flourishing a condition as I found them, and have it in my power to make a grateful return to Alexander for the kindness which in my adversity he had shown to those who are dearest to me. But if, indeed, the fatal time be come, which is to give a period to the Persian monarchy, if our ruin be a debt which must be paid to the divine jealousy, and the vicissitude of things, then, I beseech you, grant that no man but Alexander may sit upon the throne of Cyrus." And when slowly bleeding to death from wounds inflicted by his base betrayer, Bessus, satrap of a province into which Darius had fled for safety—the dying monarch begged of Polystratus, a chance attendant, for a little water: and on receiving it he said that it had become the last extremity of his ill fortune to receive benefits and not be able to return them. "But Alexander," said he, "whose kindness to my mother, my wife and my children I hope the gods will recompense, will doubtless thank you for your humanity to me. Tell him, therefore, in token of my acknowledgment, I give him this right hand," with these words he took hold of Polystratus' hand and died.

The man who could inspire such sentiments of grateful admiration into the heart of his dying enemy was more than mortal.

Plutarch tells us that Alexander, coming up at that moment, gazed with painful emotion upon the dead form of Darius. And taking the cloak from off his own shoulders he covered with it the prostrate form of his late foe, and gazing down upon the fierce dead comely face—he wept.

PHILOSOPHIES.

All the philosophies of the sleepy East and their antitheses of the aggressive West seem to have receptively influenced the myriad-minded Alexander.

Pride, not vanity, but pride essentially one with the chords of being, expressed itself in the words "And were I not Alexander I would be Diogenes." Either highest or lowest, all or nothing. Earth as kingdom or—a tub; no compromise, no half way, absolutely and unconditionally either one extreme or the other: this seeming perversity in the makeup of many men of genius has not been sufficiently considered; it is not psychologically understood; there is something humanly attractive about it; something young-world young and something old, old as the heart of man. And this perverse pride was the common link between Alexander and Diogenes, and by it each understood the other: to the former, indeed, fate awarded the earth-kingdom and to the latter—the tub; but these extremes were, by the common link, essentially one.

The Gymnosophists, or wise men of India, whom Alexander consulted, could not have deeply impressed the mind of the pupil of Aristotle, for, as Plutarch tells us, he laughed at them and sent them away with many presents.

Yet the sacrificial death of Calanus, one of these seers, could not fail to affect forcibly the susceptible mind of Alexander. Jests, dreams, auspices, oracles, theories, sophisms, philosophies, metaphysical speculations in general—well, these are agreeably adjustable; maybe so maybe not so; and when looked at too logically they can all scamper away and hide themselves elusively in Symbolism: but death, death in flames, self-sought, self-devised, self-suffered—that is real, that is awful.

On the day of his death and whilst erecting his funeral pile Calanus talked cheerfully with the Macedonians and urged them to drink deep and enjoy the passing hours. He commended himself to Alexander, whom, he said, he doubted not but that he should soon see again at Babylon. Then when the pyre was finished, he set it on fire, sprinkled himself, and cutting off some of his hair, threw it into the flame as a first-offering of the sacrifice: he then mounted the pyre, lay down calmly and covered his head in his robe. He moved not as the crackling flames drew near, nor might any one note the least tremor of fear in his limbs as the fire fed on them, nor did any sigh or moan escape from his lips: tho' what contortions of agony may have twisted themselves on his face could not be known for his head and shoulders were hid in his robe.

Alexander stood by and watched the scene. At first he thought to interpose, but learning that such was the custom of the country, and that the seer, by this sacrificial death, drew to himself high honor and special veneration from the people, he forbore. Alexander's brow was clouded as he watched the full-fed flames: in his mind re-echoed the threefold question of the Indian seer: *Whence are we come; whereby do we live; whither do we go?* Ah, whither! in his heart ten thousand recriminative contradictory questionings seethed voiceless, answerless. Alexander turned dejectedly away and retired within his tent.

That night violent reaction from the depression of the day seized upon Alexander. He ordered that all his army should rest and feast. *Carpe diem* was the dominating animus of the ensuing debauch. In a delirium of drunken joy Alexander proposed a drinking bout offering a crown to the victor. Promachus drank twelve quarts of wine and to him was awarded the prize. But Promachus did not live long to enjoy his reward, three days after he died from the effects of the debauch as did forty others who had taken part in the drinking bout at the great court feast.

There is undoubtedly a strong tendency in human nature to rush from one extreme to the other. The best by corruption become the worst; no one can fall so low as he who has been highest. But from the lowest which has known the highest there rush at times instantaneous recoil, re-ascent, re-attainment—momentary tho' it be—to the highest. Then when genius gilds that lowest, that recoil, re-ascent, re-attainment—the thoughtless world is thrilled, it listens anew, it understands.

Some of the chastest lyrics of the language have been written in recoil from, in liberation and glad bird freedom from the slough of sensuality.

The significant charm of Francis Thompson's *Hound of Heaven* lies in what it connotes rather than in what it tells. Soul-struggle is enmeshed in the lines, and defeat is heard in alto moan with every note of victory. It is the violent rebound to the height gilded, perhaps goldened, by genius.

ALEXANDER'S FEAST.

The ode *Alexander's Feast* by Dryden is one of many contributions to literature inspired by the Macedonian Madman.

>"Great genius is to madness near allied
>And thin partitions do their bounds divide."

>*—Dryden.*

Perhaps the taking of Persepolis and the mad orgy of triumph there indulged in, mark the flood-tide of Alexander's good fortune and likewise the fateful turning and re-flow of the tide. But what a tide!

Given the effects of generous wine; and the warrior, the military genius, the poet-philosopher, the dreamer of dreams, the world conqueror, the fair-haired favorite of Zeus, is, indeed, in that wondrous triumph-hour—a deity. That sycophant court-adulation, that lulling love, that music, that wine might well "raise a mortal to the skies or draw an angel down." O music, elf of a lost paradise, we remember with you, we lament, we love, we pity, we deplore, we—weep. With young-world Alexander touched to tears by old Timotheus' lyre, we too lament a bravely fallen foe:

> "He sang Darius great and good
> By too severe a fate
> Fallen, fallen, fallen,
> Fallen from his high estate,
> And weltering in his blood."

We too deplore human ingratitude:

> "Deserted in his utmost need
> By one his former bounty fed—
> On the bare earth exposed he lies
> With not a friend to close his dying eyes."

We too muse mournfully perplexed o'er all this sorry scheme of things and mingle our tears with those which thus perplexedly flowed so long ago:

> "With downcast looks the joyless victor sate,
> Revolving in his altered soul
> The various turns of chance below;
> And, now and then, a sigh he stole
> And tears began to flow."

Lyre of old Timotheus, wizard violin, symphony concert—for the hour at least, we are what you make us, and whither you lead we follow. Sadness, remorseful sorrow-love, youth and beauty caught coiled in icy death—are these, as Poe asserts, the essential elements of supreme beauty? Poe's magically beautiful *Lenore, Raven, Ullalume, Annabel Lee* confirm the poet-critic's dictum. Love in sorrow, beauty in death, mutability, vicissitude are the dominant chords in music, in literature, and in life.

But reaction follows depression, and violent activity succeeds to passivity. And this the old musician knew who played so well upon the all too humanly receptive heart of Alexander. The wail of the Grecian ghosts "that in battle were slain and unburied remain inglorious on the plain" call for vengeance and point out the abodes of the Persian gods.

Thais leads the way, and Alexander, drunk with wine and with the madness of music, follows whither she leads him; and soon the temples of the gods, the palaces of the Persian kings, the city Persepolis—are in crackling flame.

Suddenly Alexander is again Alexander. With shame of soul he sees the ruin he has wrought and frantically strives to undo what he has done. But too late; countermands clash with commands, confusion feeds the flame, Persepolis falls.

Thus culminated the triumph-banquet held in honor of Alexander's conquest of Asia and immortally sung into song by John Dryden in one of the best odes of the English language, *Alexander's Feast*.

HELLENISM.

Alexander died in a comparatively short time after the battle of Arbela and his world empire fell to pieces. What, then, was the permanent good or decisive effect of his conquests? To this question historians reply that the Hellenization of the Orient with subsequent spread of Greek culture among the Arabian Saracens, thence as vital principle re-animating the Renaissance—was the result of Alexander's conquest of Asia.

More than seventy Greek colonies were established along the route of the Conqueror. These continued to flourish long after the far seeing mind that planned them had ceased to foresee and plan. Vigorous Hellenism was easily dominant over sleepy Orientalism. And thus was bloodlessly won thro' the slow centuries, the great victory of freedom, civilization, culture, art, science, philosophy—Hellenism. From Arbela (B. C. 331) to the sixteenth century Renaissance is a conquering span that might well delight the gaze of the young warrior who once wept because there were no more worlds for him to conquer. As Napoleon's crucial defeat was not at Waterloo but in Moscow; as the British Revolutionary forces lost the colonies not at Yorktown but at Saratoga; as Carthage of old went down under world-conquering Rome not at Zama, but at the Metaurus; so the incipient death blow to Alexander was inflicted not in Babylon but at the banks of the Ganges. When his army refused to follow him any farther; when his brave Macedonians wept for their far away homes and begged to be taken back to their wives and children; when his best friends and admirers saw in the wide rolling Ganges and the enemy bristling the opposite bank, obstacles insuperable even to Alexander; when at last the Conqueror turned away unconquering, turned back, yielded—then came the fierce chagrin-humiliation, the mad beginning of the end. The world marks only the collapse-crash, but deeper insight sees sympathetically the fatal bend or twist or crack or break having in it inevitably the tragic collapse-crash.

The death of Alexander has been variously described. Some say he died of poison; others, of the exceeding coldness of the waters of the river in which he bathed; others, that his death is directly attributable to the excesses, the mad orgies of sensual indulgence into which he plunged himself as result of his chagrin at turning back from the Ganges, and of his wild grief at the untimely death of Hephaeston his favorite and friend. Doubtless the subjectivities of the various biographers have obtruded themselves over the objective reality and the simple truth will never be known. Alexander died at Babylon, 323 B. C., aged thirty-two.

CHAPTER III.
ZAMA

Had the battle of Zama been won by the Carthaginians and lost by the Romans, then Semitic influence rather than Aryan, would have moulded the civilization of Europe. These two mutually antagonistic races have grappled together in mortal combat at Zama, Tours, Jerusalem and, influentially, at Belgrade, Lepanto, Constantinople, Adrianople—and the end is not yet. Will there ever be full amity between these races?

But Rome won at Zama. And as Roman historians gravely assure us that it was better for all subsequent civilization that Rome should win, why we gratefully acquiesce; feeling, indeed, dully content that fate should, at all past times and crises, have shown herself as wisely beneficent to the winning cause as she is today. But however superior Rome may have been to Carthage, and however Roman valor, Roman dogged endurance, Roman integrity, (*Romana Fides*) may have surpassed Carthaginian—yet Hannibal, favorite of Baal, towered mountain-high over all Romans of his day, and for a time, even over all Rome.

Hannibal's personality thrills thro' the centuries. The school-boy with the good wonder-flush of admiration at the revealing vistas of the past, understands Hannibal. That eternal enmity to Rome in the son of Hamilcar; that youthful vow at the altar of Baal and its life and death fulfilment; that Herculean crossing of the Alps; Ticino, Trebia, Thrasymenus, Cannæ—Capua; Metaurus, Zama: exile, suicide—why the school-boy understands it all: and Hannibal, hunted victim of the past, is victor of the passing hour. Glamour of the historic page, generous youth, poets in prose, dreamers of dreams—and the Smoky City classroom is all aglow with white-light from the Alps as Hannibal crosses; with red light from the bloody waters of Lake Thrasymenus; with gold-glow from the rings severed from the cold dead hands of Roman knights at dread Cannæ; with mocking death-light as Hannibal defiantly dies!

CAPUA.

And after the great victory at Cannæ Hannibal led his troops into winter quarters at Capua. Here his soldiers, relaxed from the severe discipline of war and wildly delighting in the genial climate of southern Italy, gave themselves up unrestrainedly to luxuries and pleasures. And just here at Capua, in the midst of those luxuries and pleasures, lay potentially the defeat at Zama.

For the Romans, gaining courage from despair, grimly faced the fatal losses of

Cannæ, and never were the Roman people more royally Roman than when they voted thanks to the consul, Terrentius Varro the runaway loser of Cannæ,—"because he had not despaired concerning the Republic" (*quod de republica non desperasset*). Every day spent by Hannibal and his army at Capua trebly weakened his fighting force and cause as it trebly strengthened the fighting force and cause of the Romans. Capua lost Metaurus, Zama, Carthage, and Semitic dominance in Europe. *Ave Capua!*

DEFEAT.

The Roman senate determined to carry the war into the enemy's country hoping that thereby Carthage would be constrained to summon Hannibal and his army from Rome in order to defend the Carthaginian capital. Nor was this hope vain. Hannibal's eight years' success in Italy was negatived by this call from Carthage and his reluctant compliance.

Rome's ablest general, Scipio, with a well equipped army awaited Hannibal on his disheartened return into Africa. They met at Zama.

History or story relates that a personal interview between Scipio and Hannibal took place before the battle. Each stood in awe and admiration of the other: each felt mutually the charm of bravery, integrity, excellence; as men they were friends, as leaders of hostile armies, they were enemies. The interview proved futile. After a proudly lingering farewell they parted with dignity; and riding back to their respective armies prepared for immediate battle.

When the fight was fiercest and success seemed to favor the Carthaginians, suddenly the sun ceased to shine and darkness enveloped the contending hosts. It was an eclipse of the sun for which the Romans were, in great measure, prepared; the Carthaginians, wholly unprepared. Panic fear and superstitious terror seized upon Hannibal's veterans; they who had crossed the Alps, and stood knee deep in blood at Lake Trasymene and at Cannæ, yet quailed in this midday darkness.

With the slow and ghastly return of the light of the sun, Rome's bull-dogs were again ferociously at slaughter; but the Semitic heart had been smitten with awe of the unknown God; he would pray, not fight; he would fall prone in adoration of the awful Deity of darkness and of light. In vain did Hannibal strive to rouse his terror-stricken legions, in vain did he himself perform prodigies of valor: the hour of conquering Rome had come and on her way to world-conquest lay Zama. The Juggernaut of destiny rolled on, and Zama-Carthage fell to rise no more.

AND AFTER.

> "It is not in the storm or in the strife
> We feel benumbed and wish to be no more;
> But in the after silence on the shore—
> When all is lost except a little life."

—Byron.

Hannibal was only forty-five when he lost Zama. That flame of hatred toward

Rome, kindled at the altar of Baal when he was a boy of only nine years, still raged within him inextinguishably. He had lost his right eye in the Roman campaign. His brave brothers, Mago, hero of Trebia, and Hasdrubal, hero of Metaurus, had fallen in battle. The second Punic War, the war of Rome against Hannibal, or rather of Hannibal against Rome, had after phenomenal successes, ended in the disastrous defeat at Zama and in the most humiliating conditions of peace imposed upon Carthage by world-conquering Rome. All, indeed, seemed lost except a little life; yet in this dull defeat-peace, this wearily sullen after-storm, the old hate fires insatiably raged.

Hannibal, unsupported and unappreciated by his own country, passed over into Asia. He wandered from Asiatic court to court ever striving to arouse enmity towards Rome or to incite the nations to battle against her. Rome steadily pursued her inveterate foe. From court to court he passed, and from country to country passed too, the paid assassins whose sole object in life was to bring Hannibal dead or alive to Rome.

And at the court of Prusias, king of Bythinia, Hannibal was at last hopelessly trapped. Hatefully grinning faces glared in upon him from corridors, doors, windows: Rome had won.

Hannibal's presence of mind and proud dignity did not desert him even in that crucial hour, even when he toyed with death. Whilst adjusting his military robes in full presence of the leering faces at corridors, doors, and windows, he took from his finger a ring whose hollow setting contained a most potent poison. This he drank. And before any one of that self-gratulating victor-gang realized what was taking place, Hannibal fell forward dead.

The Catholic Church condemns suicide. The divine command *Thou shalt not kill* has as its complete predicate *either thyself or another*. No man can escape from God. Death only shifts the scene.

Stoicism advocated suicide; and many philosophies of the past taught that a man ought not to outlive honor.

When one considers not only the chagrin and humiliations and mental agonies, but also the rank physical tortures inflicted upon the vanquished in times past, the full meaning of *Vae Victis* (Woe to the vanquished!) is brought forcibly to the mind. Those were wild-beast times and the jungle-fights are ferocious. Plutarch speaking of the proscription list at the close of the civil war between Cæsar and Anthony says: "The terms of their mutual concessions were these: that Cæsar should desert Cicero, Lepidus his brother Paulus, and Anthony, Lucius Cæsar, his uncle by his mother's side. Thus they let their anger and fury take from them the sense of humanity, and demonstrated that no beast is more savage than man, when possessed with power answerable to his rage." And we read in Marlowe's "Tamburlaine" that this mighty despot, conqueror of many Asiatic kings, made use of these one time monarchs to draw him in his chariot: and that bridled and with bits in their mouths they fumed forward under the swishing wire-lash, while galling insults goaded on their pangs.

"Forward, ye jades!

Now crouch, ye kings of greater Asia!

* * * * *

Thro' the streets with troops of conquered kings,
I'll ride in golden armor like the sun,
And in my helm a triple plume shall spring
Spangled with diamonds, dancing in the air,
To note me emperor of the threefold world."

Whether this be only "Marlowe's mighty line", or whether it be the somewhat fantastic presentation of a dread reality—need not be known. The thoughtful student of history knows only too well just where to turn for human jungle-scenes. And there are many. From Assyrian cruelty boasting of pyramids of severed ears, lips, noses, and the deft art of flaying alive—down to Balkan-Turkish atrocities and Mexican murders the forest-way is long and dark and dreary. We hope light will yet shine upon this way. We dream that the black hags of war and of demon cruelty will not dare disport their hideousness in the future white-light. We would suspend judgment as to the past; we would not condemn Hannibal; we would play on the one-string lyre of hope—forlorn tho' it be as Watts' allegorical "Hope"—and we would wait kindly content with God's plan for this world and for a better world to come.

CHAPTER IV.
TEUTOBERGER WALD

In Germany, in the modern principality of the Lippe, may still be seen traces of the historic struggle between the Roman legions under Varus and the Germanic barbarians led by Arminius. The names "das Winnefeld" (the field of victory), "die Knochenbahn" (the bone-lane), "die Knochenleke" (the bone-brook), "der Mordkessel" (the kettle of slaughter), which still characterize various places in the gloomy Teutoberger Wald, are in themselves reminders of scenes of horror which were once dread realities; while scattered here and there may still be seen traces of the Roman camp—unmistakable evidence of the one time presence of the Roman eagles.

TRAPPED.

Perhaps all is fair in war, and the end justifies the means, and the eleventh commandment "Do to the enemy what he'd like to do to you", being altogether heartless and godless is peculiarly applicable to war: nevertheless the victory won by treachery never sounds so clarionly joyous adown the ages as the victory following a fair fight; and the deadly defeat that came by treachery has in it a pathos that redeems defeat from disgrace. Time is just.

When Varus started out at the head of his legions to quell, as he thought, an insurrection of a few unimportant tribes scattered along the Weser and the Ems rivers, Germany seemed comparatively at peace; and Arminius, the most dreaded war-lord of the barbarians, seemed to have been won over by the blandishments of the Roman camp.

It was a gala day for the troops as with ample supplies, generous baggage-wagons, plenty of camp followers, jesters, entertainers, they turned away from the frontier and plunged into the Black Forest. There was nothing to indicate that concerted action on the part of the Germans was the cause of that far distant uprising against Roman authority, and that within their ranks were half-Romanized barbarians who would desert at a given signal and use their arms against their present comrades; above all, that Arminius had secretly instigated a general uprising and that the Black Forests were blackly alive with the foe.

On went the Roman troops following their treacherous guides who purposely led them into the dense marshy depths of the woods; and when thus lost and entangled, their cavalry unable to advance, and while all the troops were called upon to construct a rude causeway over which the horses might proceed—suddenly from the gloom encompassing them on all sides came deadly arrows, missiles, javelins hurled by an unseen foe.

Varus seems to have been unable to realize that he was the victim of a stratagem. His best men, officers and soldiers, were falling around him; his cavalry slipping in slimy blood lay floundering on the way; his light-armed auxiliaries, composed in great part of brawny German youth, were slinking away and becoming strangely one with the forces whence came the arrows, missiles, javelins. Still Varus urged on the work on the causeway, and still veterans advanced to the work as veterans fell and at last the gloomy march resumed.

The attack seemed over and Varus thought some isolated tribe of barbarians had taken advantage of their hour of disability to harass them on the march. On reaching a declivity of the woody plain Varus drew up his forces as best he could in battle line and thus awaited the coming of the foe. But Arminius was not prepared to meet the Romans in battle; his rude warriors were no match for the trained Roman soldiers fully protected by helmet, cuirass, greaves, and shield. There could have been but one result to such an encounter—victory for the Romans, defeat for the cause of liberty and native land.

Arminius held in leash his blood-hounds all thro' the night. The Romans halted on the slope and, perceiving no enemy near, pitched their camp with true Roman precision and then slept long and well the heavy sleep of worn out nature that last night of mortal life.

At early dawn, while the Roman camp yet lay moveless, undreaming of the savage blood-hounds around or the deadly ambush ahead,—Arminius despatched men to the farther end of the defile with orders to fell trees and erect an impassable barricade. He then sent troops to different points of advantage on either side of the defile thro' which the fated army would advance; he gave instructions as to concerted action at the sound of the agreed-upon signal, and thus awaited the coming of morn and the renewed activities of the Roman camp.

There is something sternly terrible in the human heart which can thus joyfully contemplate the destruction of thousands upon thousands of one's fellow mortals. And yet, in this case, these Roman soldiers were the concrete embodiment of a cause which would enslave Arminius' native land, intrude deadly enervation into the integrity of a German home; and more—much more: Rome had deeply wronged Arminius, lover of liberty, lover of native land; but even more deeply had she wronged Arminius, the lover, and the man. His wife, Thusnelda, was held a captive in Rome and his child, a fair haired boy of only five years, had been made to grace a Roman triumph. Rivers of blood could not wash away such seared yet burning memories from the heart.

With fierce exultation did Arminius watch the waking of the camp, the taking up of pickets, formation of line, and the slow winding motion towards the way, the fatal way, he had foreseen they must go. Had Varus even then become suspicious of concerted treachery, he would have hastened back, would have plunged into the heart of the unknown wood, would have remained in camp, would have done anything under the sun rather than advance right into that narrow densely wooded way ambushed at every vantage point on both sides and shut in at the farther end by that barricade high as the tops of the trees. But he looked and knew not; Arminius saw and knew and exulted.

DER MORDKESSEL.

Fate is always on the winning side. As day advanced and the troops were all now fairly within the ravine, the heavens opened in streams of torrential rain. The Black Forest seemed to groan with impending doom: old Thor and Odin seemed fighting for their altars in the Druid wood, and Roman Jove was no match for this grim Teutonic Thor.

Arminius watched from the height; and just as the vanguard rounded the curve at the summit of which rose the barricade of trees, the signal for general assault all along the line arose clear and decisive from the height.

The slaughter was appalling. The bulk of the infantry, fourteen thousand men, were slain; while the cavalry which at first had numbered about eighteen hundred horsemen, partly Romans partly provincial, made here its last dread stand against the foe and—lost.

Numonius Vola, a Roman cavalry officer, seeing the utter uselessness of the attempt to continue the unfair strife, made a bold dash for deliverance. At the head of a small force, he turned away from the floundering mass of horses and men and plunged into the unknown forest. He was, however, soon surrounded by the Germans, and he and his soldiers were cut to pieces.

A brave band of Romans, last of that death-devoted multitude of men, gained a point of vantage on a hill slope and arranging themselves in a solid circle presented to the foe an almost impenetrable line of glittering points of spears. The Germans, tho' outnumbering them a hundred to one, yet quailed before that steely welcome. Perhaps, too, being themselves brave men, they were in awe and admiration of that heroic despair; perhaps, being perfectly sure of their prey, they were loth to break the savage satisfaction of gloating upon its desperation; perhaps no Arnold Winkelreid opportunely came forth to offer himself in sacrifice upon those outstretched points and so wedge open the way; perhaps, and O most dread truth-perhaps! those wild children of the Druid wood saw safely entrenched behind that helpless steel—worthy victims for Odin. And thus the night passed—that awful last night upon earth for the last of the legions of Varus.

There is an open space on the flat top of an overhanging rock, darkly terrible even today and still the favorite haunt of century old oaks: and this place tradition points out as the spot upon which human sacrifices were of old offered to Thor and to Odin. And thither the blue eyed barbarians dragged those Roman soldiers, bravest of the brave, who had stood entrenched behind their helpless steel until exhaustion overcame them and who at last overpowered by sheer force of numbers, had been taken alive by the implacable foe and dragged to the altar of sacrifice.

Strange indeed is that delusion, so often inextricably assimilable with religious fanaticism, wherein a man makes himself believe that he honors or placates Deity by immolating thereto his own enemy! Truly the human-heart god is the deification of its own desires. And that God-man upon the Cross who is essentially the everlasting antithesis of the desires of the human heart is not of man. We can understand Jove and Juno and Mars and Venus and even Odin and Thor—they are ourselves only more so: not so the Christ crucified on Calvary.

EFFECTS.

Fifteen thousand eight hundred men are estimated to have formed the army lost in the Teutoberger Wald. This irreparable loss gave to the heart of Cæsar Augustus its pathetic cry enduring even to the day of death, "Varus, Varus, give back my legions, Varus!"

Suetonius tells us that at the news of the Black Forest disaster, Augustus, in bitter grief, beat his head against the wall crying incessantly and inconsolably, "Bring back my legions, Varus": and that after many years had passed and even to the day of his death he lamented the loss as irreparable. Not, indeed, because so many men had fallen; Rome was prodigal of human life; but because his prophetic eye saw in this defeat the beginning of the end of Roman supremacy; the change of policy from aggressive to defensive; the fatal turning of a tide which should roll down upon southern Europe in inundations of desolation.

Many other ancient writers attest the seriousness of this defeat to Rome and corroborate what Suetonius says as to its effect upon Augustus. Dion Cassius says, "Then Augustus, when he heard the calamity of Varus, rent his garment, and was in great affliction for the troops he had lost, and for terror respecting the Germans and the Gauls. And his chief alarm was, that he expected them to push on against Italy and Rome; and there were no Roman youth fit for military duty that were worth speaking of, and the allied populations that were at all serviceable had been wasted away."

Florus also expresses its effects: "*Hac clade factum est ut imperium quod in litore oceani non steterat, in ripa Rheni fluminis staret.*" (The result of this disaster was that the empire which had not been content that it be bounded by the shore of ocean was forced to accept as its boundary the River Rhine).

ARMINIUS.

There was an attempt made many years ago to erect a statue to the memory of Arminius. The site chosen for this imposing monument was, of course, the Teutoberger Wald. It was suggested that contributions be received only from the English and German nations and that the statue should stand as a memorial of the common ancestry and heritage of the German-English races.

Arminius is indeed more truly an English national hero than was Caractacus, if the Saxon genealogy be properly traced.

However, the project fell through. England and Germany are not yet amicably one under the tutelage of a far off German war-lord: and no colossal statue of Arminius—successful strategist and wholesale slaughterer—rises today in gloomy Teutoberger Wald from out the dark depths of Der Mordkessel.

CHAPTER V.
ADRIANOPLE

Among the struggles of the past which seem decisively to have subverted the old order of things and ushered in the new, is the battle of Adrianople. There Valens, Emperor of Rome, was killed in battle with the Goths; and the proud Roman army hitherto deemed invincible, almost invulnerable, was defeated and destroyed.

How the wild-eyed children of the North must have gazed with astonishment upon one another as they stood victors on that field! They had not dared to hope that a Roman army would go down under their undisciplined assault; and that an Emperor of Rome should lie dead upon the battlefield was far beyond their wildest dream. Doubtless they felt within them that first awakening of brutal youth-strength: race-childhood was gone; race-manhood not yet come. And enervated old Rome; cultured, wily, effetely civilized Romans lay at the feet of these youthful, battle-flushed barbarians: and history yet hears the cries that arose as those feet advanced ruthlessly trampling.

RIVERS.

If rivers could write history—what would the Nile tell us, the Tigris-Euphrates, the Granicus-Issus, the Metaurus, the Aufidus, the Tiber, the Danube, the Moskva, the Maritza?

Mysterious Nile—with sources for ages unknown; with inundations death-dealing, life-giving; with crocodiles and alligators and implacable river God: with Theban Karnak-Luxor and the Necropolis; with Memphis and the Pyramids and the great Sphinx; with dynastic silences perturbed by a few great names—Menes, Cheops, Rameses; with the barge of Cleopatra wafted by scent-sick breezes to a waiting Anthony; with cosmopolitan bad, sad, modern Memphis-Cairo.

Tigris-Euphrates valley—cradle of the human race! home of the Accadians, a pre-historic people that had passed away and whose language had become a dead classic tongue when Nineveh and Babylon were young. Who were the Accadians? Who were the Etruscans? The Euphrates and the Tiber will not tell.

Hanging Gardens of Babylon—world-wonder: Babylon as described by Herodotus—city of blood and beauty and winged power: city surfeited with the slaughter of Assyrian Nineveh: city of the great temple of Bel: city of palaces guarded by majestic colossi—Sphinxes, winged lions, man-head bulls; city of gold and precious stones and ivory edifices and streets of burnished brass: city of the

ADRIANOPLE

fatal Euphrates, of Baltshazzar's banquet and the dread hand-writing upon the wall: city of a destruction so tremendous, so terrible that the lamentation thereof, caught vibrantly in Biblical amber, rings on and ever on adown the ages, "Babylon the great is fallen, is fallen!"

> "They say the Lion and the Lizard keep
> The courts where Jamshyd gloried and drank deep:
> And Bahram, that great Hunter—the Wild Ass
> Stamps o'er his Head, but cannot break his sleep."
>
> —*Omar Khayyam.*

And the site of Babylon, that mighty Paris of the past, is not now authoritatively known. Does the river know; does it remember the glory and the horror-night and the gloom? Is the sad sighing of rivers caused by the sorrows they see as they flow? And is the eternal moan of ocean the aggregate of the throbs of woe that the rivers have felt as they flow? Does nature know of mortal woe, does she, indeed, lament with Moschus the death of pastoral Bion, with Shelley, the untimely departure of Keats, our "Adonais"?

Fact or fancy, suggestive silence or assertive sound, poet-dream or cynic-certainty—which draws nearer to truth? which shall prevail?

Granicus-Issus—bloody outlets of the wounds of the world when Macedonian Alexander made Europe and Asia bleed!

Was Alexander the Great great? Moralize as we may, shudder at the grim bloody outlets of a wounded world; wonder at the mad folly of the masses who, at the caprice of a magnetic madman, wildly slay and submit to be slain; see clearly, in the cut and statuary past, the dolt unreason of it all, the uselessness, the Pelion-Ossa horror: yet honestly recognize that deep down in the perverse human heart there lurks loving admiration for—Alexander the Great. Rameses, Cyrus, Alexander, Hannibal, Cæsar, Napoleon—we cannot dissociate these men from their deeds; how then can we disapprove their deeds and approve these men? Why is it that a Shelley, Byron, De Musset, Swinburne, Omar—*ad infinitum*—enthrall us by the charm of their written words, even tho' we disagree with them in their tenets, their philosophy of life, their conclusions: and we censure and condemn their private lives! Can men, as Catullus sings to Lesbia, both "adore and scorn" the same object at the same time? There are many replies to these questions, but no satisfactory answer. Psychologists, take note.

The military hero, the "chief who in triumph advances", the Warrior Bold, the idols of history will continue to glimmer secure in cob-web fascination even when armaments shall have been banished from off the face of the earth and wars shall be remembered only as the myths of days that are no more. We forgive Granicus-Issus-Arbela for the sake of Alexander the Great.

And the conqueror of the world died, aged thirty-two, in Babylon. This cognizant old city and Accadian Euphrates were too wearily wise to wonder two thousand years ago. They had seen the rise and fall of many monarchs: and one more, this boy-wonder from the West, could arouse no throb of pitying surprise from scenes that dully remembered dead and gone dynasties. Why, death was old when Accadia was young ten thousand years ago; lament this stripling? No. And thus went out the conquered Conqueror of the world.

The little stream Metaurus witnessed perhaps the most momentous battle of history. Yet no magic name shines forth from that strife either as victor or vanquished. Nero, the Roman consul, victor; and Hasdrubal, brother of Hannibal, vanquished; are not the names of favorites of fame. As Byron says, of a thousand students hearing the name *Nero* nine hundred and ninety-nine recall the last Julian Emperor of Rome, and one laboriously remembers the hero of Metaurus. And yet were historians endowed with Platonic vision whereby the great is perceived in the small, doubtless the bloody conflict by the stream would be seen pivotal of history.

O hopes and fears and blasted dreams of so gigantic scale, played on a stage of Alpine eminence, no wonder you stand spectacular thro' the ages!

> "Carthagini jam non ego nuntios
> Mittam superbos. Occidit, occidit
> Spes omnis et fortuna nostri
> Nominis, Hasdrubale interemto."
>
> —*Horace.*

"Alas, I shall not now send to Carthage proud bearers of good news," said Hannibal, as he mournfully gazed at the severed head of his brother, hurled insolently into his camp, even as with impatient hope he awaited news of that brother's coming and dreamed the dream of their successfully united forces, attack on Rome, victory, and the dispatch of proud messengers to Carthage. With prophetic gaze did the hero of Cannæ see in that bloodily dead face the negation of his eight years' victory in Italy, his recall to Carthage, his defeat at Zama, his exile and bitter death, and the onward stride of world-conquering Rome over the ashes of Carthage.

Cities that have been and that are no more: Niobe-woe: rivers that know of that long ago and wearily sigh as they flow!

Old Tiber disdains the paragraph; a volume for it or—nothing.

Lordly dark Danube—so long the barrier between the known and the unknown, civilization and barbarism, the magic sun-gardens of Italy and the Teutoberger Wald!

"Varus, Varus, give back my legions, Varus"—that cry of Cæsar Augustus, Ruler of Rome, Mistress of the World, was the first wild note of a chorus of woe that arose in full diapason when Valens fell in the battle of Adrianople. From the victory of Arminius over the Roman troops under Quintilius Varus in the Black Forest of Germany (A. D. 9) to the decisive victory of the combined Gothic tribes over the veteran Roman army under Valens near the capital of the Empire, the sympathetic student of history may hear ever that losing cry of the Emperor-seer, "Give back my legions, Varus."

Legend relates that on the Roman northern frontier there stood a colossal statue of Victory; it looked toward the North, and with outstretched hand pointing to the Teutoberger Wald, seemed to urge on to combat and victory: but the night following the massacre of the Roman troops in the Black Forest, and the consequent suicide of Varus, this statue did, of its own accord, turn round and face the South, and with outstretched hand pointing Romeward, seemed to urge on to combat and victory the wild-eyed children of the North. Thus did the Goddess of Victory forsake Rome.

The Moskva river is yet memory-lit with the fires of burning Moscow; and its murmuring ever yet faintly echoes the toll, toll, toll of the Kremlin bell. Three days and three nights of conflagration—and then the charred and crumbling stillness! Snow on the hills and on the plains; white, peaceful snow healing the wounds of Borodino, blanketing uncouth forms, hiding the horror; but within the fated city, no snow, nothing white, nothing peaceful; gaunt icicle-blackness o'er huge, prostrate Pan-Slavism.

Yet surely cognizant old Moscow, secure in ruins, sighed, too, o'er the gay and gallant Frenchmen caught fatefully in the trap of desolation. Perhaps, too, the compensating lamentation of distant Berezina mingled genially with the murmuring Moskva.

Little Nap Bonaparte met his Waterloo in Moscow: history to the contrary notwithstanding.

"The soldiers fight and the kings are called heroes," says the Talmud. Of all that nameless host of ardent, life-loving men who entered Moscow, stood aghast amid the ruins, started back on that awful across-Continent retreat—the world knows only Napoleon, history poses Napoleon, Meissonier paints Napoleon, Byron apostrophizes Napoleon, Emerson eulogizes Napoleon, Rachmaninoff plays Napoleon, and the hero-lover loves Napoleon. Why? Is there any answer to ten thousand Whys perched prominently and grinning insolently in this mad playhouse of the Planets? None.

> "What hope of answer or redress
> Beyond the veil, beyond the veil!
>
> * * * * *
>
> And yet we somehow trust that good
> Will be the final goal of ill,
> That not a worm is cloven in vain;
> That not a moth with vain desire
> Is shriveled in a fruitless fire
> Or but subserves another's gain."
>
> * * * * *

The Maritza river, at one time called the Orestes river, is formed by the confluence of two unimportant streams. Adrianople is favorably situated, and ranks next to Constantinople in natural advantages.

Orestes, son of Agamemnon, built the city and gave his name both to the city and the principal river. Emperor Hadrian changed the name to Hadrianopolis

(Hadrian's city), thence our modernized Adrianople. One almost regrets that the name of the restless Orestes did not continue appropriately to designate the city of so varying fortunes and vivid vicissitudes.

Adrianople was the Turkish capital for nearly a hundred years; it was abandoned in 1453 when Constantinople came into Turkish control. The ruins of the palaces of the Sultans yet grace the ancient capital.

Adrianople is the faithful Moslem city of forty mosques. The mosque Selim II. is a close rival to Santa Sofia.

Greek and Macedonian, Roman and Byzantine, Christian and Moslem, Turk and Bulgarian, influences have in turn dominated the city of three rivers; each re-baptizing it with blood: and the end is not yet.

In 1713, Charles XII. of Sweden was a guest in the castle of Tumurtish. Little then did the valiant Madman of the North dream how ignominiously his own meteoric career would close: little did he see himself as fixed in fame, not by his combats and victories, not even by his gallant defeat at Pultowa, but by being the inspiration in the moralizing mind of Dr. Samuel Johnson of the following lines:

"He left a name—at which the world grew pale—
To point a moral or adorn a tale."

The Vanity of Human Wishes is indeed exemplified not only in Charles XII. of Sweden, but also in many other favorites of fortune: not one of whom, perhaps, but would add to or alter his own peculiar setting in fame—if perchance he should be able to recognize himself at all in the historic figure masquerading under his name. How seldom does it chance that the world honors a man for what that man feels to be his best title to honor?

Would Julius Cæsar, red-hand conqueror of Gaul, know himself as the Shakespearean hero? And Nero, Louis XI., Wallenstein, Henry VIII., Roderick Borgia—would they claim even passing acquaintance with themselves as fame has fixed them? If these men took any of their fighting qualities with them into the Spirit Land, there must have been some flamy duelling when they met their respective biographers.

And so the blood of battle bathed Adrianople one thousand five hundred and thirty-five years ago and—last year (1913). And we talk learnedly about the defeat and death of the Roman Emperor Valens, and of the effect of that victory upon our respected barbarian ancestors with consequent doings of destiny, etc., etc.—because we *don't know*: and we say little about the Servian-Bulgarian-Turkish capture of Adrianople last year, because it is too near and—*we know*. Then, too, who can poetize or moralize or even sentimentally scribble over the yet hideously bleeding wounds of war? When they are healed, when the moaning is still, the mangled forms moveless, the cripples on crutches gone, the lamentations silenced, the last-lingering heartache soothed in Death—why, then, perhaps; but not now. Battle in the real is a human butchering: and there is no other delusion under the sun more diabolically sardonic than that which makes animal savagery seem patriotism and the red-hand slaughter-man a hero. From the Homeric Hector-Achilles, deliver the world, O Lord.

Strange, indeed, is the contrariety between the real of War and the ideal, the far away hero and the near Huerta, the blood spilled and stilled and the bright life-blood spilling, the sorrow silenced and the agonized cries that arise, the battle of Adrianople, 378 A. D., and the siege and capture and re-capture of Adrianople (1912-1913).

CHAPTER VI.
CHALONS

If, in the battle of Chalons, Attila and his Huns had been victorious over the combined forces of the semi-Christianized Visigoths under Theoderic and the Romans under Ætius—then Hungvari influence rather than Teutonic would have dominantly determined the progress of the civilized world.

Rome had fallen: effete in her withered hand lay the rod of empire: and swarming about her, now quarrelling among themselves and with her, now fraternizing, but always more or less in awe of her prostrate majesty were her barbarous children—Franks, Burgundians, Alans, Lombards, Gauls, Alemanni, Visigoths, and Ostrogoths. These had known Rome in the hour of her pride and power; they revered the Rome that was for the sake of the Rome that had been; they had imbibed something of her culture, her military discipline, her laws, her religion. Semi-civilized, semi-Christianized, with the bold Teutonic virtues yet pristine from the Black Forests of Germany,—they were the possible material of an excellence surpassing that of Rome, even when Rome could boast of excellence.

But about 450 A. D. hordes, innumerable hordes, *velut unda supervenit undam* (even as wave upon wave) of hideously ugly, lithe, little, wiry, imp-like men poured into Europe from the Asiatic lands north of the Black Sea. By their numbers, their lightning-like rapidity, their uncanny appearance, and their brute ferocity, they quickly swept the countries before them, put to flight the Alans, the Ostrogoths, and other tribes dwelling along the course of the Danube, and finally under their terrible leader Atzel (Attila), Scourge of God, they confronted the civilized and semi-civilized world in arms on the plain of Chalons.

BATTLE.

From early dawn even until darkness frowned over the field the blood-feast flowed: and Death was satiated.

Attila withdrew to his camp. He left an effective guard around his wagons and outposts and made every thing ready for a prolonged and obstinate resistance to the attack anticipated at early dawn. Nevertheless he built for himself a massive funeral pile, placed upon it his most valued treasures and his favorite wives, and was fully prepared and resolute to apply the torch, ascend the pyre, and so perish in the flames—should defeat fall to his fortune on the following day.

Morning dawned. The awful work of death on the preceding day appalled both armies; miles upon miles of outstretched plain lay covered with carnage;

CHALONS

the all-night-writhing mounds of men were ominously still. Sullenly did foe gaze upon foe; but each recoiled from renewal of the slaughter.

Still the advantage was with the allies; for Attila, so late the fierce aggressor, was barricaded in his camp—tho' grimly awaiting attack indeed, and prepared to resist to the end and die like a lion in his den.

Did the Romans know of that funeral pile? They may not, indeed, have known the peculiar manner in which Attila would seek death, but they knew that he would die by his own hand—if the worst came. Cato had done so and Varus and Brutus and Cassius and Hannibal and Anthony and Cleopatra—*ad infinitum*.

Addison, in his tragedy *Cato*, has graphically portrayed the conflicting thoughts and emotions in the mind of a man who feels that life cannot longer be borne and yet shrinks back from the horror and the dread unknown.

Cato had lost the battle of Utica. He had been true to Pompey, he had fought the last battle for the cause of Pompey—and lost. And Cæsar was indeed god of this world, and the morrow held no place on all this so vast earth for Cato; this lost-battle night must end it all. He read Plato's discourse on the immortality of the soul, and in the lines of Addison, thus soliloquized:

> "It must be so. Plato, thou reason'st well:
> Else whence this pleasing hope, this fond desire,
> This longing after immortality?
> Or whence this secret dread and inward horror
> Of falling into naught? Why shrinks the soul
> Back on herself and startles at destruction?
> 'Tis the divinity that stirs within us;
> 'Tis Heaven itself that points out an hereafter,
> And intimates eternity to man.
>
> * * * * *
>
> The soul, secured in her existence, smiles
> At the drawn dagger and defies its point.
> The stars shall fade away, the sun himself
> Grow dim with age and nature sink in years;
> But thou shalt flourish in immortal youth
> Unhurt amidst the war of elements,
> The wreck of matter and the crash of worlds."

But Attila did not mount his funeral pile. The day passed without attack upon Attila's formidable position. King Theodoric lay dead upon the plain and his son Prince Thorismund, who had distinguished himself in the battle, was victoriously proclaimed King of the Visigoths.

Ætius, Valentinian's able general, held in leash both the Romans and the Visigoths even while Attila slowly broke up camp and withdrew in long lines leading northward.

EFFECT.

The effect was that of victory for the allies. Rome was saved from a fresh infusion of barbarism whilst her Teutonic element was still semi-barbarous. The German characteristics—love of liberty, independence, and reverential regard for women—thus dominated the Christian civilization which now began to flourish vigorously out from the decadence of pagan Rome.

If, as Byron says,

"Cervantes laughed Spain's chivalry away,"

then also it may be said that Lucan laughed Rome's gods and goddesses away. The laugh is the most insidiously potent of all destructive forces when the laugher is loved and the times are attuned to hear. Not satire, not personal bitterness, not even the withering invectives of a Juvenal are as sweepingly effective as the quills of ridicule, the inescapable miasma of the laugh. Once let the grin distort the frown of Zeus and majesty trembles, awe smiles, reverence dies.

And so the pagan deities were dead; their temples empty and meaningless; and thundering Jove and jealous Juno and murderous Mars and all the other deifications of the all too human heart of man were impotently silent under the spell of the solemn central figure of the new religion—Christ on the Cross.

And the Church in the name and with the power of that sublime Sufferer taught the reverse of all that paganism had taught; of all that the world had hitherto heard and heeded; of all that the all too human heart of man held as dearest and best. "Love your enemies," said the Church to the men who had fought at Chalons. "Blessed are the merciful, Blessed are the clean of heart, Blessed are the peacemakers", reiterated the Church to her semi-barbarous children. And they understood only in part, and they did deeds of appalling atrocity even while acquiescing to her teachings: for the will to do good was, indeed, emotionally present with them, but the power so to do failed them crucially. Yet their sins were of surface-passions not of the inmost heart; for they were ever in reverential awe of the sublime Sufferer on the Cross; for he spoke as no man ever yet had spoken, and he lived what he said, and he died praying for his murderers: and all this is not of man—as none knew better than they who knew the naked human heart.

ATTILA.

History has not done justice to Attila. History has not done justice to any lost cause. For the winners, not the losers, are the writers as well as the makers of history, and all forces combine to make them unjust to the lost cause.

Herodotus gives us the story of Marathon, Thermopylæ, Platæa, Salamis; Persia had no Herodotus: Homer extols the exploits of the Grecian army, the valor of Achilles; but Hector had no Homer: Roman historians tell the story of the Punic wars; Carthage from her desolate site sown with salt cares not what they say, whilst Hannibal, bravest of the brave, and supreme military genius, speaks on the historic page only from the lips of the hated Romans.

When Protestantism finally won in England and the long able reign of Elizabeth established it firmly upon a political basis, then were fulminated against the

CHALONS

Church of Rome all those unjust accusations and gross misrepresentations which, crystallized in history and in literature, seem ineradicable as fate. But truth is older than history or literature, and more analytically powerful than the synthetic forces of crystallization, and patiently prevalent even over fate.

Elizabeth's very legitimacy depended upon the establishment of Protestantism in England and the overthrow of Catholicity; and to this two-fold end the energies of the very astute daughter of Henry VIII. were undeviatingly directed.

It takes about three hundred years from the time of a cataclysmic upheaval of any kind before the minds of men can view it dispassionately or estimate it without bias. But what are three hundred years to age-old Truth?

Elizabeth possessed, in addition to the terse Tudor qualities, the rare gift of foresight. She knew the power of the pen and the possibilities for fame or infamy in the men of genius of her time. And so her court was open to the great men of that day and her smile of patronage was ever ready to welcome poet, artist, dramatist, politician, warrior, traveler, historian, and statesman: she became all to all and she won all.

As *Gloriana* in Spenser's immortal "Færie Queen" she reigns forever. Bacon, Spenser, Sidney Smith, Raleigh, Voltaire—as Voices having a thousand echoes throughout the years—have amply rewarded that patient foresight and have fixed her in fame as—what she was to them—Good Queen Bess.

And so Attila and his Huns in low long sinuously winding northern lines left behind them the carnage strewn plain of Chalons, and the camp with its ominous pyre, and the dazed foe. And thus victory remained to Ætius, last of the Romans: and the field of Chalons which saved civilization and semi-civilization from an untimely intrusion of rank barbarism; which secured domination to the Teutonic race rather than to the Sarmatic; which freed Europe from Asia—was the last victory of imperial Rome.

Attila died two years later; some say as the victim of poison secretly mixed with his food by Ætius' ever vigilant spies. With him his vast empire passed away: and the leader who once claimed as proud titles,—"Atzel, Descendant of the Great Nimrod. By the Grace of God, King of the Huns, the Goths, the Danes, and the Medes. The Dread of the World"—died ignominiously one carousal wedding night: and history, ever unjust to a lost cause, writes his name among the *Almosts* and calmly commends the destiny by which Attila and his Hunnish hordes were defeated in the great battle of Chalons.

CHAPTER VII.
TOURS

The battle of Tours had as result the dominance of the Aryan race over the Semitic in Europe; and of the Cross over the Crescent throughout the world. As Gibbon says speaking of the phenomenal conquests of the followers of Mohammed: "A victorious line of march had been prolonged above a thousand miles from the rock of Gibraltar to the banks of the Loire; the repetition of an equal space would have carried the Saracens to the confines of Poland and the Highlands of Scotland; the Rhine is not more impassable than the Nile or Euphrates, and the Arabian fleet might have sailed without a naval combat into the mouth of the Thames. Perhaps the interpretation of the Koran might now be taught in the Schools of Oxford, and her pulpits might demonstrate to a circumcised people the sanctity and truth of the revelation of Mahomet. From such calamities was Christendom delivered by the genius and fortune of one man." (Charles Martel).

Persia, Lydia, northern Africa, Spain, had successively fallen under the devouring zeal of the fanatics of the desert. Hot and arid and consuming as the sun o'er yellow sands was the inspiration of the Prophet fire-breathing thro' the Koran. "The sword," says Mahomet, "is the key of heaven. A drop of blood shed in the cause of God is of more avail than two months of fasting and prayer; whoso falls in battle, all his sins are forgiven; at the day of judgment his wounds shall be as resplendent as vermillion and odoriferous as musk." Hearts thus athirsting aflame had as their dream-goal, their vermillion glory—the conquest and subjugation of the city of the Cæsars, the city of the Church, Rome, Immortal Rome.

From the Bosphorus to the Gibraltar glowed the victor Crescent with extremities burning into Europe. Unsuccessful on the Bosphorus but successful on the Gibraltar, Spain was soon enveloped in its fanatic fire and its flame-tongues darted over the Pyrenees.

The Saracens of Spain were commanded by Abderame, favorite of the caliph Hashen, victor of many fields, idol of the army, and devout believer in the promises of the Prophet. Abderame was proud of his battle scars, not yet indeed resplendent as vermillion and odoriferous as musk, but potentially so and cherished accordingly. He would yet slay "many cut-throat dogs of misbelievers" and so gain more vermillion. One is here tempted to say, in the words of Virgil describing the sacrifice of Iphigenia,

> "Learn thou then
> To what damned deeds religion urges men."

TOURS

Too bad that the word "religion" must needs do service to express the extravagances of mythology, the ravings of fanaticism, and the teachings of the gentle Christ.

Eudes, duke of Aquitaine, first opposed the Moslems as they advanced beyond the Pyrenees. He was at first successful but later suffered a signal defeat at Toulouse, "in so much so", says an old chronicler, "that only God could count the number of Christians slain." Eudes himself escaped and hastening northward sought the aid of Charles, duke of Austrasia, mayor of the palace, and soon to be known as Charles Martel (Charles the Hammer.)

On came the conquering Saracen hosts, grown insolent by victory, deeming themselves invincible, and proudly confident in the destiny that should lead them to Rome. Asia and Africa were in arms against Europe; the old against the new; maturity against lusty youth; and they met steel to steel on the plains of Tours.

> "He either fears his fate too much
> Or his deserts are small;
> Who dares not put it to the touch
> And gain or lose it all."

Tours towers in solemn awe in the vague *What might have been*. Was it wise to have risked Christendom on the issue of one battle? The result says Yes; but—

Upon what seeming trifles turns the hinge of destiny! The casting-vote of Callimachus, urged by the eloquence of Miltiades, made Marathon; panic-fear let loose among Darius' million men made Arbela; an eclipse of the sun won at Zama; Teutoberger Wald, Chalons, Tours—invisible, unknown, but not the less effective were the forces in these fights making fatefully for defeat and for victory. That which we term a trifle may be as a single bead of perspiration; trifling in itself, no doubt, but representative of a force far from trifling.

Battle raged indecisively all day long from early light till dark. Prince Charles seemed to wield the hammer of Thor. Abderame fell. The Saracens withdrew sullenly within their tents. Quiet darkness gathered mournfully over the living, the dying, and the dead.

And the next morning there was a great silence in the Moslem camp; in so much that the Christians trembled as at some uncanny treachery and stood awaiting they knew not what. But as the early morning hours passed and broad daylight brought back manly courage, the Christian army approached the camp of the enemy. It was deserted. The foe had fled. Christendom had won.

Charles did not immediately pursue the fleeing Moslem hordes. He still feared treachery. Perhaps, too, some wakening sentiment of humanity restrained him from further bloodshed. The vast plains of Tours were covered with ghastly forms horribly hacked and hewed but now strangely still. According to an old chronicle the number of Moslem dead upon the field of Tours was three hundred and fifty thousand; that of the Christians, fifteen hundred. Surely that was enough of slaughtering death even for Karl Martel.

The battle of Tours was fought Oct. 4, 732 A. D. The following Spring Charles went in pursuit of the Saracens who were still ravaging southern France. They withdrew from place to place as Charles drew near; and ultimately—without risking another encounter with the Hammer of Thor—they retired across the Pyrenees. France was freed from the Crescent.

THE EIGHTH CENTURY.

All writers agree that the eighth century was the darkest age of the so-called Dark Ages. The Benedictine monks, authors of *L' histoire litteraire de la France* say that the eighth century was *the darkest, the most ignorant, the most barbarous* that France had ever seen. It seemed to be the seething culmination of four hundred years of Barbarism, one infusion following fast upon another.

In 407 A. D. the Vandals from the upper Rhine invaded Gaul and Germany: in 410 the West Goths under Alaric besieged and sacked Rome: in 429 the Vandals under Genseric came down upon Numidia and Mauritania: in 443 the Burgundian invaders settled on the upper Rhone and on the Saone: in 451 came the Huns under Attila. Towards the end of the fifth century the Franks from the lower Rhine came into Gaul, destroying every vestige of civilization that had survived the invasion and occupation of France by the Vandals and Burgundians. About this time, too, the Angles and Saxons established themselves in Britain, and the Visigoths in Spain. In the sixth and seventh centuries the Heruli, the East Goths, and the Lombards destroyed whatever remained of Roman civilization in northern Italy.

And now to complete this scene of chaotic confusion came the fanatic Moslem hordes from the south. Surely every remaining reminder of old-world civilization seemed about to be crushed and broken to pieces between these contending crest waves of barbarism. The cataclysmic clash and crash came at the battle of Tours.

THE CHURCH.

William Turner, S. T. D. in his History of Philosophy speaking of the eighth century says: "We can scarcely realize the desolation that during these centuries reigned throughout what had been the Roman Empire. Although surrounded by all the external signs and conditions of dissolution and decay, the Church remained true to her mission of moral and intellectual enlightenment, drawing the nations to her by the very grandeur of her confidence in her mission of peace, and by the sheer force of her obstinate belief in her own ability to lift the new peoples to a higher spiritual and intellectual life. It was these traits in the character of the Church that especially attracted the barbarian kings. But, though towards the end of the fifth century Clovis became a Christian, it was not until the beginning of the ninth century that the efforts of the Church to reconquer the countries of Europe to civilization began to show visible results. The Merovingian kings—the 'do-nothing-kings,' as they were styled—could scarcely be called civilized. Even Charlemagne, who was the third of the Carolingian dynasty, could hardly write his name."

The Church is for all ages and all conditions of men. She is equally effective in answering the soul-questionings of savage peoples, barbarous, semi-civilized, cultured, and æsthetic: of a superstitious monk of the Thebaid and of the philosopher Augustine, Bishop of Hippo: of a Thais of the desert and of Ursula, virgin and martyr: of Charles Martel, of the bloody battle Tours, and the gentle Francis of Assisi: of Constantine, Clovis, Charlemagne; and of John Henry Cardinal Newman, Mangan, Oscar Wilde, Strindberg, and Francis Thompson. As the manna that fell from heaven for the Israelites had in it every taste that might be in accordance with the peculiar desire of him who tasted, so in like manner, the Church of all ages has ever brought to her children that which was in accordance with their peculiar needs and desires. Fiercely kind, sternly kind, firmly kind, humanly kind, and divinely kind—as occasion may require, the Church has been and may be.

In Charles Martel, hero of Tours, the Church had a gallant defender. Under his son Pepin, and his greater grandson Charlemagne, the Church made that leap forward, away from ninth century barbarism, up and onward to her fair and full flowering in the thirteenth century Renaissance.

GREEK FIRE.

At the second siege of Constantinople, when Moslemah with a land force of one hundred twenty thousand Arabs and Persians stood ready to attack the city; and a fleet of eighteen hundred ships—as a moving forest,—covered the Bosphorus, Constantinople seemed doomed. A night attack of the combined land and sea forces was planned; and no one might reasonably doubt the issue of the conflict. But here again the unexpected happened.

Truly the race is not to the swift nor is the battle to the strong. Marathon, Salamis, Arbela, Tours, Cressy, Poitiers, Agincourt, Saratoga, Valmy,—were battles not to the strong. "There's a divinity that shapes our ends."

As night approached and the formidable "moving forest" gathered round the doomed city, suddenly there darted amidst the towering timbers—lighted monsters, Greek Fire-ships belching forth from dragon-mouthed prows the fatal Greek Fire. Here, there, everywhere plunged the fire-breathing ships leaving behind them Moslem vessels in flames. The Bosphorus was on fire. Of the fated soldiers in that mighty fleet of eighteen hundred ships, few escaped to make known the tragedy or to describe the horribly magnificent scene.

What was the Greek Fire? how compounded? how used? how propelled? does the world of today know the secret of Greek Fire? Gibbon says: "The historian who presumes to analyze this extraordinary composition should suspect his own ignorance and that of his Byzantine guides, so prone to the marvelous, so careless, and, in this instance, so jealous of the truth. From their obscure, and perhaps fallacious, hints it should seem that the principal ingredient of the Greek Fire was the naphtha, or liquid bitumen, a light, tenacious, and inflammable oil, which springs from the earth, and catches fire as soon as it comes in contact with the air. The naphtha was mingled, I know not by what methods or in what proportions, with sulphur and with pitch that is extracted from evergreen firs. From this mixture, which produced a thick smoke and a loud explosion, proceeded a fierce and obstinate flame, which not only rose in perpendicular ascent, but likewise burnt with equal vehemence in descent or lateral progress; instead of being extinguished, it was nourished and quickened by the element of water; and sand or vinegar were the only remedies that could damp the fury of this powerful agent, which was justly denominated by the Greeks the *liquid* or the *maritime* fire. For the annoyance of the enemy it was employed, with equal effect, by sea and land, in battles or in sieges. It was either poured from the rampart in large boilers, or launched in red-hot balls of stone and iron, or darted in arrows and javelins, twisted round with wax and tow, which had deeply imbibed the inflammable oil; sometimes it was deposited in fire-ships, the victims and instruments of a more ample revenge, and was most commonly blown through long tubes of copper which were planted on the prow of a galley, and fancifully shaped into the mouths of savage monsters, that seemed to vomit a stream of liquid and consuming fire."

The paralyzing effect of fear let loose among a multitude of men has decisively determined many a battle. When the Romans saw elephants for the first time, and saw them too, in the midst of Pyrrhus' hostile hosts bearing down upon them—those brave world-conquerors promptly turned and fled. Chariots armed with scythes madly rushing down upon a body of infantry, were used with success by the Britons against Cæsar's terrified legions. And Greek Fire, Byzantium's secret for four hundred years, infused such enduring terror into the hearts of the nations that had taken part in that night attack upon Constantinople, that this remembering fear, rather than the effective force of Byzantium, may be said to have saved Christendom.

By the defeat of Tours in the west and the failure of the siege in the east, the two horns of the Crescent, burning into Europe, were effectively repulsed and chilled. Mohammedanism with its threefold blight—propagation by the sword, polygamy, and religious intolerance—was swept back into Asia, leaving Europe to develop under the milder sway of Christianity.

Writers of note are unanimous in attributing to the victory of Charles Martel over the Saracens at Tours the deliverance of Europe from the thraldom of Mahomet. Even Gibbon so characteristically fond of "Snapping a solemn creed with solemn sneer" speaks of this battle as "the event that rescued our ancestors of Britain and our neighbors of Gaul from the civil and religious yoke of the Koran." Arnold speaks of this victory as "among those signal deliverances which have effected for centuries the happiness of mankind." The historian Ranke writing of this period points out as "one of the most important epochs in the history of the world, the commencement of the eighth century, when on one side Mohammedanism threatened to overspread Italy and Gaul, and on the other the ancient idolatry of Saxony and Friesland once more forced its way across the Rhine. In this peril of Christian institutions, a youthful prince of Germanic race, Karl Martell, arose as their champion, maintained them with all the energy which the necessity for self-defense calls forth, and finally extended them into new regions." Schlegel, with devoutly grateful heart, tells of this "mighty victory whereby the arm of Charles Martel saved and delivered the Christian nations of the West from the deadly grasp of all-destroying Islam."

CHAPTER VIII.
HASTINGS-SENLAC

"If you can keep your head when all about you
Are losing theirs and blaming it on you:
If you can trust yourself when all men doubt you
Yet make allowance for their doubting too.
If you can wait and not be tired by waiting,
Or being lied about don't deal in lies;
Or being hated not give way to hating,
And yet don't seem too good or talk too wise."

— *Kipling.*

IF.

If—laconic fate-word! hinge of destiny! *If* the Persians had won at Marathon; and if the brilliant imagination of a Persian Herodotus had fixed in fame the glories of conquering Persia: *if* the Peloponnesian War had not mutually destroyed the Grecian empire: *if* Alexander the Great had lost the battles Granicus, Issus, Arbela; *if* world-conquering Alexander the Great had been successful in the conquest of his own down-dragging human heart, and *if* he had not died at Babylon, aged thirty-two, world-victor and self-victim: *if* the village by the Tiber had not advanced by bloody strides o'er fixed-star battlefields from Rome a wilderness, to Rome Mistress of the World: *if* the barbarous hordes of the North had not ever longingly before their eyes the fairyland of southern Europe, the troll-gardens of Italy: *if* Rome had not become enervated; *if* Gaul and Goth and Hun and Norseman had not won: *if* the Crescent had waved victorious o'er a fallen Cross at Tours, Belgrade, Lepanto: if William of Normandy son of Robert the Devil, had been pierced by an arrow and buried indistinguishably among the dead on the slaughter-field of Senlac-Hastings—If!

But we are a perennially hopeful race and happily unimaginative and dully content with the Real: and so we unquestioningly acquiesce when grave historians tell us that in each and every historic struggle the juggernaut determinant of the *If* acted favorably to the best interests of civilization and progress: so, too, would we obligingly believe had the determinant favored the opposing cause. Perhaps to all-conquering Progress as to world-conquering Rome, all battles are victories; either as a victory proper with roll of triumph-drum and flash of conquering colors, or as that grim Cannæ-defeat potential of a future Zama-victory.

It is well that there should be two possible interpretations of the answers of the oracle: thus is Truth ever serenely secure unperturbed by the errors of mortals.

PEGASUS.

It is hard to control the winged steed. His next flight and whereabouts of alighting are as happily unknown to the rider as to the beholder—to the writer as to the reader. However Pegasus, the real, can never fail to be interesting whether he leap over the historic ages, or play antics on an *If*, or neigh irreverently in the temple of Delphian Apollo, or speed to the finding of Harold Godwin amid the indistinguishably dead on the slaughter-field of Senlac-Hastings.

ROLLO THE DANE.

Vikings of the northern seas, wolf-men of the Sagas, dark devotees of Thor, heirs of Valkirie—little wonder that the semi-civilized world shuddered at their distant approach; little wonder that Charlemagne, hero of a hundred wars, grew sick at heart, foreseeing the rivers of blood that should deluge fair France, when, one day, by chance, his eagle gaze caught sight of the Dragon-Head long-boats of the Northmen as yet far off, red-glittering on shaggy northern seas.

Time passed; the Charlemagne vision had dread realization; France, England, Southern Europe were overrun by conquering Saxon, Dane, Norsemen.

And Rollo of Norway, called Rollo the Dane, settled in northern France. He named that part of the country Normandy in honor of his native land. After many years of bloodshed and as advancing age subdued the battle fever, he entered into a compromise compact with Charles the Simple of France. Rollo was to do homage to the king, be baptized, and marry Giselle, the king's daughter: in return he should be acknowledged as the lawful Duke of Normandy with right of succession to his heirs forever. But rough old Rollo protested against the humiliating conditions of the homage ceremony. It was obligingly agreed that it should be done by proxy. History relates that the warrior appointed as proxy in the homage ceremony felt deeply the humiliation of having to kiss the slippered foot of King Charles and that in this act he rudely raised the foot so high that the monarch was unseated and fell from his chair. Amid the wild hilarity caused by this scene and the seeming revival of barbarism, King Charles was too fearful of Rollo to make open complaint: concealing his chagrin he proceeded with the ceremony and no doubt felt happily relieved when all was over, and Rollo at the head of his wild followers stood forth as Robert, the first Duke of Normandy. The baptism and the marriage followed in due succession and thus was won over and fixed in civilization, Christianity, and historic fame Rollo the Dane, forefather of six dukes of Normandy, and of a long line of English kings extending directly or indirectly from William the Conqueror to Queen Anne, last of the Stuarts.

WILLIAM OF NORMANDY.

William was the son of Robert, sixth duke of Normandy: William's mother was Arlotte, a peasant girl, daughter of a humble tanner of Falaise. William was reared at the court of his father, and being a beautiful and precocious boy as well as heir apparent of the realm, he became a great favorite among the warrior courtiers of Duke Robert.

The magic of danger, the lure of the unknown, the glamour of romance and chivalry lay, at that time, in a pilgrimage to the Holy Land. Thither turned the eyes of the half-civilized descendants of the savage old Vikings; and, as the war fever of youth abated, many men, combining incongruously remorse for crimes and penitential expiation with love of daring adventure, turned away from strong feudal castles and lordly possessions in Europe to brave the hardships and uncertainties of a pilgrimage to the Holy Land. Among those thus lured into fatal uncertainties was Robert le Diable, sixth Duke of Normandy. He left the realm to his son William—if by chance he himself should not return—appointed Alan of Brittany regent during William's minority, and having left the boy safe at the court of Henry of France, Robert set out on that pilgrimage to the Holy Land from which he never returned.

Ever insatiably hungry is the heart of man. Pleasure is a mirage. Yet perhaps, happier is it to fall and perish in full pursuit of an ever receding pleasure than to walk inane in the beaten sand-way and—live. To do is easier than to endure: to act is easier than to wait; to roam abroad and strive is easier than to stay at home and pray; to wander amid strange scenes and stranger men, to draw the approving sword in a cause approved, to fight and die and leave his bones to bleach on Asiatic plains were easier far for Rollo's blood than to wait and waste away secure in a feudal fortress of Normandy.

At Robert's death there were various claimants to his possessions; but, finally, owing, in great measure, to the fidelity of the regent Allan of Brittany, the dukedom was secured for William. He left the court of Paris, and soon after, taking full possession of the realm, he began to exhibit those indomitable character qualifications which together with his military education and robust physical powers led him on from conquest to conquest even unto the tragic culmination at Senlac-Hastings from which he came forth blood-baptized as William the Conqueror.

THE LADY EMMA, PEARL OF NORMANDY.

When Ethelred, the Saxon King of England, fled from his realm and left it to the victorious Danes, he sought refuge at the court of Richard, the fourth duke of Normandy. There he met and married the Lady Emma, sister of Duke Richard. This lady was famed for her beauty and known throughout the realm as the Pearl of Normandy.

Edward of England, known in England as Edward the Confessor, was the son of Ethelred and Lady Emma; and it was upon this relationship that William, at the time of Edward's death, laid claim to the crown. Whatever may be said of this claim, it was at least more tangible than that of Harold, son of Earl Godwin.

The days have gone by when the rights of blood relationship were claims for which contending realms might squander fortunes and armies: but he who estimates the ages past by the standards of today, would better roll up and read no more the enigmatic scrolls of history. Rivers of blood have freely flowed in order that some royal rascal, slightly richer in royal rascality than a rival claimant, might win a throne. Yet we who cannot understand the code of the *Samurai*, as worked out logically today; we to whom the principles of *Bushido*, when carried to the last full measure of devotion, are fascinatingly unreal; we to whom *jun-shi*, *hari-kiri*, *seppuku* are words ominous, indeed, but unintelligible even when translated into deed in the white light of today[1] — how shall we be able to understand or estimate aright the mysteries of the mighty past!

So upon this faint claim of relationship, William, the seventh duke of Normandy, nephew of Lady Emma, Queen of England, founded his right to the English throne: and for better or worse, right or wrong, faint claim or no claim — he won.

MATILDA OF FLANDERS.

William sought to strengthen his position by an influential matrimonial alliance. Matilda, daughter of the Duke of Flanders, became the object of his choice. This lady was very beautiful and an adept in the accomplishments of her time — music and tapestry weaving. In fact a wonderful piece of tapestry known as the Bayeaux Tapestry and even now in a state of comparative preservation, is said to have been the work of Matilda of Flanders, wife of William the Conqueror. This famous piece of embroidery on linen is four hundred feet long and nearly two feet wide; it is a series of designs illustrating the various events and incidents of the Battle of Hastings and other exploits of the Conqueror.

William and Matilda were married in 1052, the Battle of Hastings was fought in 1066, so that the Bayeaux Tapestry has resisted the gnawing tooth of time for more than eight hundred years.

Who shall unerringly perceive in the glare of the passing day, what is great, what small: what is enduring, what evanescent! Linen fibres, silken threads, a woman's needlework — endure: shields, helmets, swords, battle axes, all the iron horrors of Hastings have passed away.

And the moral values of the passing hour are, to human perception, equally elusive, intangible, untraceable. But are we called upon to understand the full meaning of the passing show?

Surely the Power above us smiles at our endeavors to fit together here in Time things whose fitness shall not have developed in a thousand years.

The old Norse story runs that when Thor went to Jotun-heim, the home of the Giants, he failed ignominiously in the accomplishments of the tasks imposed upon him. He struck with might and main at the head of the prostrate giant Skrymir, but the huge creature only moved restlessly and murmured in his sleep that a leaf or twig had fallen upon his face. Thor failed in the race with Hugi. Thor failed in the drinking bout proposed by Utgard-Loki. Thor failed in the wresting match with Elli, the old nurse of Utgard-Loki. Thor failed to lift the Giant's sleeping cat, and though he tugged with all his strength, he succeeded in lifting only one paw from

---

[1] Death of General Nogi.

the ground. Thor failed apparently in every task that was set before him.

But, behold! when revelation was made, it was found that Thor had, indeed, been Thor and that his failure-achievements had terrified even the Norns. For the giant Skrymir later confessed to Thor that by magic he had shielded his head with a mountain when Thor struck with his hammer, and that the mountain had been well nigh severed by the blow. And as to the race with Hugi, why Hugi is Thought; and no man may hope to surpass the speed of thought. And as to Thor's failure in the drinking bout, why the drinking horn had been secretly in connection with the ocean, and Thor's deep draughts had seriously lowered old ocean's vast domain. And as to Elli, the nurse, why she was Old Age and her no mortal may overcome. And as to Thor's failure to lift the sleeping cat—why the seeming cat had been in dread reality, the Midgard serpent coiled around the world, and his nearly successful efforts to rouse the serpent and tear it from the charmed circle, had terrified even the Norns. And so Thor was still Thor in his failure-achievements in Jotun-heim: so likewise may we, in the great Revelation, be found to have been splendid conquerors in the grim failure-strife of Time. And then, too, shall a fateful Skrymir make known to us the true nature of the forces against which we strove; the fatal necessity of failure in such a strife, were we Thor or even Odin: then too shall we learn with astonishment and delight the Herculean results of our labors; and throughout all the upward cycles of our immortality we shall be stronger and better because of our failure-achievements down in earth's Jotun-heim.

MONASTERIES.

As there was some tie of consanguinity between William and Matilda, their marriage could take place only by special dispensation from the Pope. After some vexatious delays, however, this dispensation was obtained, but William and Matilda were advised by the Pope to erect a Hospital for incurable patients and two monasteries, one for men, the other for women.

William and Matilda joyfully agreed to fulfill these conditions. The hospital was built first, and later two imposing monastic piles, one under the special patronage of Matilda, the other under William, were erected at Cæn. Strange to relate that after forty or fifty years had passed away, Matilda was brought to her wedding monument monastery and quietly interred, and a few years later William was laid to rest in his wedding monument monastery. And thus near yet apart they have slept thro' the long ages.

HAROLD GODWIN.

Harold Godwin and William of Normandy were not strangers to each other when they drew up their battle forces on the field of Senlac-Hastings. Harold had spent some months in Normandy at the court of William some years prior to the death of Edward. And William had made known to Harold his claim to the English throne and his intention of maintaining that claim when the time should come. History relates that Harold, concealing his own ambitious designs, vowed solemnly to support William's cause.

At the death of Edward, however, Harold found himself at the head of a powerful Saxon faction and felt strong enough to oppose William, should he persist in his intent to claim the throne.

But what about that oath made solemnly in the presence of the Sacrament! Is a man ever courageously self-respecting and invincibly valiant in whose soul festers the ulcer—perjury! When Richard the Third went forth to battle upon Bosworth field, he was already defeated and slain by his own avenging conscience.

When Harold heard of the landing of William's Norman troops at Pevensey, he was then in the north of England engaged in a struggle with the Danes under the leadership of his own brother Tostig. Harold was slightly wounded in this battle but, in the end, Tostig lay dead upon the field and the Danes were put to flight. Thus from a battlefield red with a brother's blood, Harold, a wounded man and a perjured man hastened southward to his fate in the dread slaughter of Hastings.

> "And were things only called by their right name,
> Caesar himself would be ashamed of fame."
>
> —*Byron.*

The word *battlefield* is a euphemism for human shambles. And "the chief who in triumph advances" is, in grim reality, but the lustiest and the bloodiest of the dogs of war. And the Alexanders, Caesars, Napoleons are the madmen who have made men mad by their contagion, and have so accumulated horrors Pelion-Ossa piled on horrors as to make the angels weep o'er this mad planet of the universe.

A forceful peculiarity of mental unsoundness is the vehemence with which its victim conceives himself to be right and everybody else wrong, himself sane and all not in agreement with him insane. This fatuity is characteristic of ages as well as of individuals. It is manifest in the complaisant superiority which every age, every generation assumes toward the immediately preceding. "Back in the past, during the Dark Ages, in primitive times, etc." are the words of balm with which the passing hour begins its own eulogy.

But blood is blood and hate is hate and war is war, whether waged by Macedonian Alexander B. C. 331, or by the Balkan forces A. D. 1912. Shades of the fallen upon that age-long battle ground! wouldn't you feel strangely at home in the fray if by any chance you should come to life today?

International courts of justice, arbitration, disarmament, World-Peace—will they ever prevail? Knowing the past, knowing the heart of man, we answer *No*: dreaming of the future, dreaming of the godlike in the heart of man, we answer *Yes*.

So all day long the tide of battle rolled—from early day till dark. And William and his Norman followers were in possession of the field, and round them lay a host of dead and wounded, yet by reason of the sudden darkness and the exhaustion of the troops, no search could be made even for the Norman wounded: and tho' groans and cries of thirst and deep sighings arose incessantly from the writhing masses just darker than the darkness, yet no search could be made or any aid given by reason of the utter exhaustion of the troops.

And on that field of death and awfully dying life Harold Godwin lay happily dead under a heap of the slain. Two monks, lanterns in hand, went out to search for him and with them went also the mother of Harold and Edith the woman that loved him. After hours of fruitless search amid scenes of gruesome horror, and as the dawn burst in red wonder over a bleeding world, Edith discovered Harold. So changed was he, so mutilated, hacked and hewed, blood-clotted, dismembered, that even his mother knew him not but the woman that loved him knew. With great difficulty was the body of Harold extricated from under the heap of the slain, but the monks and the women persevered at their task and finally bore him away.

WILLIAM THE CONQUEROR.

We know only what life has brought within our own cognition; beyond that all is conjecture. The love turned to hate and delighting in the avenging pangs of a lover is utterly uncognizable by the man or woman unto whom love is love forevermore. Dante Gabriel Rossetti's weird poem "Sister Helen" is, thank God, quite meaningless to the greater number of women: and yet such women as Sister Helen exist; they know each other; they understand the poem.

Strange, indeed, was that practice among primitive people, of injuring an image of an enemy and claiming that thereby, in like manner, they injured the enemy. In the poem referred to, the woman is engaged in the magic rite of holding a waxen image in the flame and letting it slowly consume under incantation. She is interrupted from time to time by her wondering little brother, and in her answers to him Helen makes known her wrongs, her slighted love, her love turned to hate, her revenge, her vindictive madness, her black-art vengeance reaching even beyond the grave, her triumph-despair. At the end of the incantation as for the seventh time she turns the waxen figure and it breaks up and melts dripping away—her perjured lover dies.

A formula of this magic rite runs as follows:

"Take parings, nails, hair, saliva, etc., of your victim and make them up into his likeness with wax from a deserted bees' comb. Hold the waxen image in slow flame for seven consecutive nights repeating intently over the image—

'It is not wax that I am scorching,
It is the liver, heart, spleen of *So and So*.'

After the seventh time, turn your figure and your victim's life will go out with the last drippings of the wax into the flame."

Gladly would we relegate this grotesque rite back to the twilight of animistic superstitions: but if we are vitally in touch both with the past and with the passing hour, we dare not do so. There is subtle relationship between this concretely hideous formula of other days and such abstract expressions—not unfamiliar today—as *mental assassination*, use of *malicious animal magnetism*, hypnotic control of the aura, aggressive telepathic forces, etc. The garb of the occult changes, adapts itself with Protean pliability to the passing hour—but the inscrutable Occult forever hid behind the Isis-veil, does not change.

It is said of Molière that behind the mask of comedy, he bore a heart heavy with tragic woe: that his farces are satires on human nature: that he, more piercingly than any other mortal, had gazed down into the heart of man. Perhaps for Molière then, or such as he, the all around understanding of every act or emotion is sympathetically possible, but to the ordinary mortal there is full knowledge only of that which has come within his own cognition.

Therefore, to depict the feelings of William the Conqueror, as he stood among the dead and dying on the field of Hastings is beyond the power of ordinary mortal. Whether he felt elated or depressed—for we know that ofttimes in the hour of seeming triumph there is deadly depression of soul; whether he turned heartsick from the reproachful glare in dead and dying eyes and shuddered that such things should be, or gazed delightedly and eagerly upon the sullen silent faces of the Saxon foe: whether with infinite pity regretful and remorseful he could have wept for the brave men who lay dead because of him, or saw them not at all, or, at best, only as stepping stones to a throne: who shall say? who shall know?

When a man as stoically severe as the late General Nogi, has by chance been revealed to the world as a tender father and a man weighed down by fatal woe even whilst he was urging on the furiously victorious death-charges up the hill of Port Arthur—we would willingly suspend judgment as to what may have been the feelings in the hour of triumph deep down in the heart of William the Conqueror.

ROBERT'S REBELLION.

William had left his wife Matilda as regent of Normandy when he set out for the invasion of England. Robert, the eldest boy, a bright lad of fourteen and his mother's idol was also participant in the regency. As the years rolled by and the boy grew more able and willing to rule, Matilda willingly sank to second place in active government and Robert was in deed if not in title the Duke of Normandy.

Eight years passed by before William found his English realm calm enough for him to leave it and make a visit to his old home Normandy. At his coming he found all going on admirably without him. Matilda was happy in the affection of her favorite son Robert; and Robert a valiant young prince, was happy in the love of an over-indulgent mother and the possession of ducal power. All this was changed when William came. Perhaps jealousy of the place Robert held in the affections of Matilda, perhaps insatiable avarice and lust of power, perhaps unnatural hatred of the son who dared to oppose the unconquerable will of the Conqueror—perhaps any or all of these feelings intermingling impelled William to act as he did, but certainly, in the light of calmer times, William's conduct towards his son Robert cannot be justified.

Robert was deposed from the place which he held during the regency and which he had slowly grown to regard as his own. The proud spirit of the princely youth could not endure this humiliation. He fled to Flanders, and there among his mother's friends and his own followers and retainers, he gathered together an army and appeared in open rebellion against his father.

Matilda was, indeed, a devoted wife to William, but she was an even more devoted mother to her son; and her heart was torn with grief when hostilities broke out and father and son were arrayed against each other on the field of battle. It is related that Robert saved William's life in the engagement that followed. Both were in armor and their faces were concealed by the helmet and visor, so that they did not recognize one another. In the heat of the strife, Robert saw one of his knights hurl a javelin at a burly figure on horseback in the opposing ranks. With a cry and a groan the injured man fell from his horse, and Robert horrified at the voice which he recognized as his father's, rushed headlong to the side of the fallen man and rescued him from the feet of trampling horses. He was touched with remorse and wept as William uplifted his helmet and visor revealing a face white and weary and covered with blood.

The generous heart of the youth even then might have been won to better things had William himself been morally high enough to draw his son higher; but he was not.

That hasty action and as hasty reaction in the hearts of the young-world children—hate surging suddenly into remorseful love, strength into weakness, audacious rebellion into repentant submission: and then as hastily surging back again! Robert saving the life of his father against whom he had come in battle array: Richard Cœur de Lion bitterly weeping at the bier of his father whose death he had desired and hastened: Henry I. who never smiled again after the loss of his son and heir when the *White Ship* went down: the Black Prince, chivalrously subservient to his prisoner King John of France conquered at Poitiers—strangely fascinating is this hasty action and reaction in the hearts of the young-world children!

Matilda succeeded in bringing about a reconciliation between her husband and her son after that strange battle; but it was only for a time. William was compelled to return to England and Robert took advantage of this occasion to enforce his claim on Normandy. Matilda was secretly in favor of her son (the women are always right!) tho' she tried to conciliate both. Rebellion again raged in Normandy openly carried on by Robert and secretly abetted by Matilda. William was, at the same time, threatened with an uprising in England and was obliged to remain on the island. But certainly there could have been little peace or happiness in the heart of the man whose subjects were in insurrection against him and in whose household there was hate and discord and rebellion.

As William became more and more alienated from Robert, he looked more favorably upon his second son William Rufus and his third son Henry. These in turn succeeded him upon the throne of England to the exclusion of Robert, the rightful heir.

Robert languished in prison the last twenty-seven years of his life—thus adding another chapter to the book in which is recorded the story of men and women who have nearly succeeded in their ambitious designs—but not quite: the *Almosts* of literature and of life; who have struggled fearfully and failed; whose fierce activities have died down in dungeon gloom; who have been, in the main, more sinned against than sinning; who have lived and happily died leaving behind a tragic name flame-cut into fame.

EXEUNT OMNES.

Matilda died in 1082, and about five years later William followed her to the tomb. Matilda died in the palace part of the monastery at Cæn erected by William at the time of their marriage. Her last days were deeply shadowed by the renewal of hostilities between William and Robert, and by the death of a daughter, a young and beautiful girl full of hope and promise, who had suddenly been stricken with an incurable illness.

It was well that in those days in the twilight of the grave, Matilda could not foresee the sad fate of her son Robert. Little did that tender mother-heart dream of the destiny overhanging the boy, when at that last clandestine interview she hastily blessed him and kissed him good bye. Thank God for the heavy curtain rolled down impenetrably between the present and the future.

William, notwithstanding his grievance against Matilda, came to see her in her last illness. He was with her when she died. He followed her in the funeral cortege to that monastery built by her in far off happier days, and he stood sadly by as that devoted wife and mother of his many children was laid to rest.

Philip of France abetted the cause of Robert, and William, now an old man and grown excessively corpulent, was forced again to take up arms. William was under medical treatment for his corpulency, and Philip, hearing of this, jestingly remarked that "the old woman of England was in the straw." A tale-bearer repeated this to William and in a rage the King swore that "the old woman of England would soon make things too hot for him." William kept his word; burning villages and war horrors arose on every side as the irate monarch began his march of revenge.

The town of Mantes, on the road to Paris, was in flames, and William, riding thro' and giving out orders in all directions, failed to notice that his horse was treading upon smoking ashes. Suddenly the horse reared violently, his feet evidently having been burnt by smouldering flame, and William was internally injured. He was borne by litter to a monastery just outside the gates of Rouen. William soon realized that he was face to face with the King of Terrors. He shrank with horror from the remembrance of his deeds: he ordered that a large sum of money should be given to the poor and that their prayers should be enlisted in his behalf; he gave orders that all the churches of Mantes, destroyed by him, should be at once rebuilt, and he richly endowed the monastery.

His sons William and Henry were soon at his side, but Robert came not. When asked as to whom he bequeathed the kingdom of England he replied that it had not been bequeathed to him, that, therefore, he bequeathed it to no one, but that he wished that his son William Rufus might succeed him.

William, at last, when he could hold it no longer, left Normandy to his eldest son Robert.

William tried to make his peace with Heaven as the dread summons came nearer and nearer. He was one morning suddenly aroused from a comatose state by the ringing of the church bells. Hastily arising and thinking himself in the clash of battle he demanded to know what that clangor meant. On being told that it was the church bells of St. Mary's ringing for morning services, he lifted up his hands, turned his eyes heavenward, and exclaimed, "I commend myself to my Lady Mary, the holy Mother of God." He then sank back and died.

William Rufus succeeded to the throne of England and after a troubled reign of thirteen years, he died.

Henry, the youngest son of William the Conqueror, claimed the crown and after overcoming his brother Robert in a terrible battle, he quietly took possession of the throne. Robert was held a prisoner by Henry I. until death released him twenty-seven years later.

So long ago were these scenes enacted, and so very long have the actors slumbered! Would they recognize themselves in the descriptions given of them today? and would they be pleased or displeased with the parts attributed to them in the play?

However all the actors, immediate and mediate, connected with the battle of Senlac-Hastings have long ago gone off the stage. The colossal *If* upon which once hung the history of England has become fate-fixed actuality. The Houses of Plantagenet, Lancaster, York, Tudor, Stuart—England's story from 1066 to the passing hour are inseparably woven one with the battle of Senlac-Hastings and the *If* determinant in favor of William the Conqueror.

CHAPTER IX.
ORLEANS

What France won in three years (1428-1431) under the leadership of Joan of Arc restored all that France had lost during the Hundred Years' War. Cressy, Poitiers, Agincourt were negatived by Orleans.

More wonderful than any myth of any nation under the sun, than any concept of poetic fancy throughout all literatures, than any vision of poet-sage or seer in all Sybilline rhapsodies—is the plain historical narrative of the life and deeds of Joan of Arc. Some power beyond the natural worked thro' the peasant maid of Domremy.

"The people of Orleans when they first saw her in their city thought that it was an angel from Heaven that had come down to save them", said an eye-witness of the scene who testified at the reversal of Jeanne's sentence ten years after her death. On the contrary the Duke of Bedford, in a letter still extant, writing to Henry VI. and lamenting recent disasters to the English army says: "And alle thing there prospered for you til the tyme of the Siege of Orleans taken in hand God knoweth by what advis.

"At the which tyme, after the adventure fallen to the person of my cousin of Salisbury, whom God assoile, there fell by the hand of God as it seemeth, a great strook upon your peuple that was assembled there in grete nombre, caused in great part as I trowe, of lakke of sadde beleve, and of unlevefull doubte, that they had of a disciple and limb of the Feende, called the Pucelle, that used fals enchantments and sorcerie."

> "So certainly
> As morn returneth in her radiant light
> Infallibly the day of truth shall come"

said the Maid of Orleans.

That day of truth has come. Around Joan of Arc the charmed circle of the Church of Rome is drawn. Let no man dare to call evil that which the Church calls good; let no man dare to attribute imposture, hysterical exaltation, or necromantic might to one whom the Church calls Blessed. Vindicated, rehabilitated, restored, cherished, Blessed is now the Maid who died five hundred years ago burned at the stake as a witch.

Condemned by the University of Paris, an ecclesiastical tribunal? Yes. Hounded to the stake by Pierre Cauchon, Bishop of Beauvais? Yes. But the Church can shake off and disclaim the clinging hands of her children whose touch pollutes her; and the Church of all ages can outshine the lurid darkness of any one age, and deprecate, and deplore and denounce the deeds done in that lurid darkness. Splendidly, too, and with stern magnanimity, defying apparent self-contradiction, can the Church reverse the decrees of ecclesiastical tribunals, and stoop down to pick up and restore and rehabilitate and bless a strangely foolish child whom kings and courts and the great University of Paris had condemned and cast away.

The Church of the Middle Ages must ever stand darkly enigmatic to the non-Catholic student of history. He cannot rightly appreciate the binding force of spiritual authority. The withering away from fear of Church censure, the clinging claim upon all the powers of the soul in the prayers and ceremonies and sacraments of the Church, the isolating horrors of her excommunications, the abject fear of her spiritual punishments, powerful alike over prince and potentate and peasant—are practically meaningless to the non-Catholic.

That scene in "Richelieu" by Sir Edward Bulwer Lytton, well illustrates the power of the Church in the Middle Ages. King Louis XIII. has sent to demand that Julie de Mortemar, Cardinal Richelieu's orphan ward, shall be immediately sent to the court subject to the king's pleasure. The girl clings to the Cardinal for protection. To these messengers Cardinal Richelieu replies,

"To those who sent you!—
And say you found the virtue they would slay
Here couched upon this heart, as at an altar,
And sheltered by the wings of sacred Rome.
Begone!"

They go. But soon again comes Baradas, favorite of the king, First Gentleman of the Chamber, and about to be made premier to succeed the temporarily deposed Cardinal Richelieu. To Baradas' insolent importunities the eloquent old Cardinal in righteous wrath exclaims:

"Ay, is it so?—
Then wakes the power which in the age of iron
Burst forth to curb the great and raise the low.
Mark where she stands!—around her form I draw
The awful circle of our solemn Church!
Set but a foot within that holy ground,
And on thy head—yea tho' it wore a crown
I launch the curse of Rome!"

Baradas abashed retires, the king's suit ceases; the Church has triumphed.

LA PUCELLE.

France is assuredly a genius-mad nation: whether genius or madness shall ultimately prevail is an answerless question. The Republic shall go down in "a slough of mire and blood" is the current prophecy today; but, then, France has gone down in mire and blood many and many a time and, phœnix like, she has risen and soared aloft led onward and upward by some strong Genius-Child.

Joan of Arc and Napoleon Bonaparte stand unique in history; each picked up torn, bleeding, fragmentary France and restored her to her rightful place in the family of nations. That Napoleon Bonaparte, a man, a soldier, and a master of opportune occasion, should have rescued France is not wonderful; but that the Maid of Domremy, a timid girl aged seventeen, who "knew not how to ride or to handle a sword", whose hand never shed blood, should have, amid most inopportune occasion, prevailed in battle against Talbot, Gladsdale, Falstofe and the flower of the English Army is, past all credence, wonderful.

France as a nation was extinguished by the Treaty of Troyes. Isabeau of Bavaria, wife of Charles VI. deliberately and exultantly aided the trembling hand of the imbecile king as he signed away his kingdom. Henry VI. of England, infant son of Henry V. and Catharine, daughter of Charles VI. of France, was proclaimed heir of the united kingdoms France and England: later, at the death of Henry V. this child was crowned at Paris king of England and of France. Isabeau of Bavaria aided in the coronation ceremony, graciously accepting young Harry Lancaster as king of France to the exclusion of the rightful heir, her own son, Charles the dauphin.

As Schiller says:

"Even the murderous bands
Of the Burgundians, at this spectacle
Evinced some token of indignant shame.
The queen perceived it and addressed the crowds,
Exclaiming with loud voice, 'Be grateful, Frenchmen,
That I engraft upon a sickly stock
A healthy scion, and redeem you from
The misbegotten son of a mad sire.'"

Surely the first part of Merlin's prophecy had been ominously fulfilled: France was lost by a woman. Would a woman save France? And far away—among the wooded hills of Domremy wandered the splendid Dreamer who should, in three bright, bitter years—flame-cut into fame forever—undo what Isabeau had done, throw off the incubus of alien authority, negative the Treaty of Troyes, and save France.

Thank God for the enthusiasts, for those who follow their Voices! Tho' their way lies thro' adamantine opposition, they know it not, their eyes are fixed on the goal; and even as one in hypnotic somnambulism leaps on from toppling crag to crag unawed by the sheer depths of yawning destiny o'er which he strides, so do these enthusiasts press on to the goal: and they reach it.

Joan appeared at the camp at Blois, clad in a new suit of brilliant white armor, mounted on a stately black war-horse, and with a lance in her right hand, which she had learned to wield with skill and grace. Her head was unhelmeted; so that all could behold her fair and expressive features, her deep-set and earnest eyes, and her long black hair, which was parted across her forehead and bound by a ribbon behind her back. She wore at her side a small battle-axe, and the consecrated sword marked on the blade with five crosses which had at her bidding been taken

ORLEANS

for her from the shrine of St. Catharine at Fierbois.

A page carried her banner which she had caused to be made and embroidered as her Voices enjoined. It was white satin, strewn with fleurs-de-lis; and on it were the words *"Jhesus Maria"*. And thus spectacularly equipped Joan made her appearance at Orleans at the head of an enthusiastic French army. The astounded English soldiers could only stare and glare; and had it not been from their greater fear of their irate commanders, these brave heroes of Agincourt would have promptly run away in panic fright from this dread Maid.

Joan advanced towards the besiegers and solemnly admonished the English generals to desist from their unlawful holding of Orleans, to withdraw at once from France, and to spare further bloodshed. Oaths and imprecations and ribald jests answered her earnest abjuration. Joan returned to her ranks and gave order for battle. Yet she shrank from the fury of the strife and her heart recoiled and sickened at the sight of suffering and death. Joan's most trustworthy biographer tells us that her own hand never shed blood.

Joan was wounded at the battle around Orleans; an arrow from a cross-bow penetrated her armor between the neck and shoulder and remained fastened in the wound. Joan grew faint from pain and she suffered La Hire to lead her from the fray. Recovering herself in a little while, she sat up and withdrew the arrow with her own hands, then putting a little oil on the wound, she mounted and galloped back to where the battle was raging. Joan's presence reinspired her followers; mad dash after dash was made against the fort held by Sir John Gladsdale. The English soldiers, thinking her to have been mortally wounded, were terrified at her abrupt return. Again Joan called out to Gladsdale to surrender and spare further bloodshed. With an oath the infuriated general came out upon the drawbridge shouting orders for a final desperate assault. As he stood thus conspicuous between the two armies, a cannon ball from the town crashed thro' the drawbridge and Gladsdale fell and perished in the waters. At the sight of this disaster, and also at the attack upon the fort under the leadership of Joan in person, the English army fled. The siege of Orleans was raised. The long imprisoned Orleannais came forth and hailed Joan as their deliverer sent from Heaven.

CHARLES VII.

The raising of the siege of Orleans was quickly followed by the decisive battle of Patay in which Talbot, the English commander, was wounded and taken prisoner together with a large part of the English army. The way now lay open to Rheims. Thither marched the victorious French forces under Joan of Arc carrying with them the perplexed and irresolute Dauphin. In the cathedral at Rheims, July 17, 1429, with all the solemn ceremonies of the coronation of kings, this weakling was crowned Charles VII. of France.

Perhaps as the son of an imbecile sire and Isabeau of Bavaria, Charles VII. couldn't help being what he was. So in the shadow of that comfortable Lombrosian theory we leave without reproach the man whom, in the good sunlight of common sense and honest manhood, we should scathingly reproach as dastard and ingrate.

After the crowning of Charles at Rheims, Joan desired to withdraw from the king's service and go back to Domremy. She declared that her work was done; she, moreover, maintained that her Voices no longer urged her to remain in the field, or pointed out unerringly just what she should do. Du Nois and La Hire prevailed upon her to remain with the army.

Joan was wounded in an unsuccessful attack upon Paris. And the following spring in a sortie at Compeigne Joan was taken prisoner by the Burgundians and subsequently sold to the English.

Joan was cast into prison at Rouen. Here the indignities to which she was subjected, as related by her biographers, are almost incredible. The apathy of the fickle French towards their late "deliverer sent from Heaven", and the dastardly indifference of Charles VII. during her imprisonment and throughout her trial and death form a conspicuous page in the black book of Human Ingratitude.

Et tu, Brute! (And thou too, O Brutus!) cried Cæsar as he fell pierced, indeed, with twenty-three wounds, but slain at the sight of his beloved Brutus among the murderers. That was death in death. *And if my enemy had done this to me, verily, I could have borne it. But thou, my friend and my familiar!*—This agonizing cry—shrieked so that all the world may hear by Cæsar, Wolsey, Joan—rises in bitter silence in many a heart. Only those we love have power to wound us; and we stand defenceless, unresenting, dim-wondering, yet loving. Nancy of the slums under the murderous blows of Bill Sykes, Cæsar as he gazes at Brutus, Joan of Arc blessing Charles VII. from her Calvary of flames—shine as radiant silhouettes of human nobility on the somber overshadowing background of human ingratitude.

JOAN'S VOICES.

"This pure, this gentle creature cannot lie!
No, if enchantment binds me, 'tis from Heaven
My spirit tells me she is sent from God."

—Schiller.

Both the French and the English firmly believed that Joan of Arc was aided by some preternatural power; but was she borne upward by "airs from heaven or blasts from hell"? Burned at the stake as a Witch, Relapsed Heretic, Accurst—thus died the Maid whom the Church has raised to her altars.

But ere we too scathingly condemn that scene, disgraceful alike to the Church and to human nature, which was enacted in the Rouen market-place May 31, 1531; it might be well to turn a balancing gaze upon our own Cotton Mather madness which had its orgies upon Gallows Hill, Salem, June-September 1692. Nor are we of the passing day and hour sufficiently washed white of the soot of Occultism that we may conspicuously disclaim the witch-burning at Rouen. In the late Christian Science rupture accusations of "mental assassination" and the use of "malicious animal magnetism" were mutually charged. Just what that may mean in the esoteric circle, I know not; but full meaning and full knowledge would doubtless ramify back to Rouen.

> "There are more things in Heaven and Earth, Horatio,
> Than are dreamed of in your philosophy."

Yes, infinitely more: all that the human eye can see or the ear hear or the intellect know is but as a shore-lapping wave of the infinite ocean of the Seen, the Heard, the Known. And what if some eye be abnormally endowed with vision, or some ear be attuned beyond the normal for hearing, or some finely fashioned intellect transcend ordinary knowing—shall it not inevitably see more or hear more or know more of that infinite ocean? and shall it not fearlessly and fully make known what it sees or hears or knows? And then what? Why we gregarious Little People, spitefully content in limitations, will with consenting conscience, condemn the witch to death.

Joan's Voices spoke to her more especially when the church bells were ringing; they were mild and very kind; they always spoke soothingly. When their music stilled she lay prostrate upon the ground and wept because they had left her behind; because she had not been able to ascend with them and go home to that waiting Heaven. Joan's Voices urged her to become the saviour of France. And when the child remonstrated that she was only a poor peasant girl and did not know how to ride a horse or handle a sword, the Voices insistently replied, "It is God who commands." And then the Maid arose and went forth on that mighty mission.

Orleans, Jargeau, Troyes, Patay, Rheims, Laon, Soissons, Compeigne, Beauvais were her victories. Then came the rapid flame-way of her own emancipation.

As Joan stood bound to the stake, and as the smoke and flames were hiding her from the *vulgus profanum*, a wild-eyed monk advanced to the pyre. He held aloft a large iron cross having upon it an ivory figure of the tortured Christ. A look of infinite sympathy and love lit up the eyes of Joan as they rested upon the Christ. Her lips parted in prayer. Blessings upon Charles VII., prayerful petitions for her beloved France were heard thro' the crackling flames. Not once did her eyes turn from the tortured form upon the cross; thence was coming the strength that enabled her to bear the pangs of death, thence, too, the grace which urged her to pray for her murderers.

Round her rolled the fire; her long black hair was blazing, her head, her face, her wondrous eyes were flooded in flame. All was ending. But the monk held aloft the Crucifix. A gust of wind parted the fire, again the charred eyes rested upon the tortured form on the cross, her lips moved in prayer; and again she was lost in flames. Thus perished Joan of Arc, aged nineteen, virgin and martyr.

Take not the ivory Christ away. 'Tis sorrow's mutual friend; 'tis the strength of strong agony; 'tis the sympathizing consoler of the rack, the stake, the prison house of pain, the dim valley of the Shadow, the Rouen sea of flames. The Crucifix understands.

Pan? Well, yes, for the bright blue Arcadian hour in young-heart Arcady. But for the gray every day and the solemn night; for the hours of pain and loss and parting and change, sickness, old age, sorrow; for the crucial crises of life as they come in bitter pangs to us of a lost Arcady; for the mother whose boy fell at Vera Cruz; for a Joan of Arc in the flames—ah! take your grinning Pan away; we want the Crucifix, we want the thorny crowned Christ who has suffered and understands.

Ten years after the death of Joan, there was a judicial reversal of her sentence of condemnation. Twenty-five years later the Church instituted a thorough investigation of Joan's claims, deeds, trial, condemnation, and death. The process and results of this inquiry may be found in detail in the work "Proces de Condemnation et de Rehabilitation de Jeanne D'Arc," published in five volumes, by the Société de L'Histoire de France.

Many eminent English authors, besides innumerable French biographers, have written in deep sympathy with Joan of Arc; among them may be mentioned Southey, Hallam, Carlyle, Landor, de Quincy, Lang, and our own Mark Twain. Voltaire's vulgar burlesque-epic is now generally regarded as an insult to France and a superficial satiric calumny. Schiller in The "Maid of Orleans" distorts well known historical facts.

In 1869 Mgr. Dupanloup, Bishop of Orleans presented at the Vatican his petition and claims for the beatification of Joan of Arc. The trial proceeded slowly, but on April 11, 1909, Pius X., the present reigning pontiff, pronounced the decree which raised Joan to the first step in the process of canonization. She was solemnly declared Blessed. "A Mass and Office of Blessed Joan taken from the *Commune Virginum* with 'proper' prayers have been approved of by the Holy See for use in the diocese of Orleans." Joan's canonization is now under active consideration.

CHAPTER X.
LEPANTO

Cross or Crescent! We of the present time can form no adequate idea of the import couched in those words in mediæval time. Strange that rivers of blood should flow in the interests of the cause of the Prince of Peace! Would the Christ,— who, dying upon the Cross prayed for his murderers,—have it so? Perhaps over his friends even more pitifully than over his erring inimical world the sublime impetration unceasingly ascends *Father, forgive them for they know not what they do.*

And Allah "the mild, the merciful, the compassionate"—where was he that tragic Sunday morning October 7, 1571, when one hundred thousand of his followers, singularly lacking in his characteristic qualities, stood red-hand in slaughter! Alas for the ideal when fitted to the real: it is shattered; its shimmering iridescence dies down gray and dead.

TO FIGHT OR NOT TO FIGHT.

The Ottoman empire, flushed by a long series of successes under Solyman the Magnificent, had grown insolently aggressive. The memory of Tours and of Belgrade no longer acted as a deterrent to the fierce victors of Constantinople; their eyes were ever turned longingly toward western Europe, and their dreams were of bloodshed and victory.

The island Cyprus belonged to Venice, but its situation made it highly desirable as an Ottoman possession; and upon the old principle that might makes right—a principle unfortunately ever retaliatively new—the Turkish forces besieged Cyprus. The town Nicosia, capital of Cyprus, fell an easy prey, and the atrocities committed on the defenceless inhabitants horror-thrilled the Christian world. Later the town Famagosta after a prolonged and obstinate resistance was captured but under circumstances of peculiar malignity. In the words of Prescott: "While lying off Cephalonia Don John received word that Famagosta, the second city of Cyprus, had fallen into the hands of the enemy, and this under circumstances of unparalleled perfidy and cruelty. The place, after a defence that had cost hecatombs of lives to the besiegers, was allowed to capitulate on honorable terms. Mustapha, the Moslem commander, the same fierce chief who had conducted the siege of Malta, requested an interview at his quarters with four of the principal Venetian captains. After a short and angry conference, he ordered them all to execution. Three were beheaded. The other, a noble named Bragadina, he caused to be flayed alive in the market place of the city. The skin of the wretched victim was then stuffed: and with this ghastly trophy dangling from the yard-arm of his galley, the brutal monster sailed back to Constantinople, to receive the reward of his services from Selim (son and successor of Solyman)."

Submit to that? Wait apathetically for the Turks to come to Venice, Rome, Madrid and do in like manner? Well, no; not in the real, whatever may be the ideal. What then? Why, *Fight*.

Non-resistance: and if thine enemy smite thee upon the cheek, turn to him the other also; and if he take thy coat give to him also thy cloak; love your enemies; do good to them that hate you and despitefully use you: and as result, what? Crucifixion. A nation of Christs would be put to death as unjustly as was the Christ of Calvary.

Fortunately or unfortunately—we know not which it may prove to be—only the Tolstoyan few will carry to their logical conclusions the principles of non-resistance; and few, if any, even of the Tolstoyan few, will abide by these conclusions and stand calm, kind, compassionate, even under the fatal final Injustice. The great body of men, of today as of every other day of the long ages of time, defend their rights; and if that defence means that blood must flow,—then let it flow. And all the more freely will blood flow and all the more sternly indomitable will be the strife when men feel themselves justified as they strike the blow; when they feel themselves called upon to conquer or to die for a cause that they hold just; when they fight elated and fortified with the assurance that they stand as bulwarks warding off the concrete embodiment of all that they hold evil from all that they hold dear and good.

"The bravest are the tenderest,
The loving are the daring."

Some of the bravest and the tenderest of men have trodden knee deep in human blood. There have been wars just and inevitable; and what has been may again be. We hope not; we dream not; the Peace Palace of the Hague looms spectrally on the future horizon; we are looking that way: and at times this Peace Palace seems assertively real—ready to cope with armaments and with red-hot wrongs; but again it rises fancifully and floats evanescently away and fades on a gray sky. Is it Mirage?

THE CHRISTIAN KNIGHT.

Next in moral excellence to the Christian martyr is undoubtedly the Christian knight.

Chivalry—fair flower of Feudalism, night blooming cereus wide opening in white splendor exuding fragrance in somber mediæval midnight! King Arthur and his Table Round; knights errant done to death by Don Quixote and yet victors even over the smile; Chevalier Bayard, the knight without fear and without reproach; Richard Cœur de Lion, the Black Prince, Lohengren, Parsifal, Siegfried, Don John of Austria—are flowerets of that Flower caught wax-white in amber and fixed fadelessly.

In all the sweep of history from Egypt to the hour, there is nothing nobler than the ideal Christian knight. To stand in awe of the omnipotent God; to go about the world redressing human wrongs; to love with young-world love bashfully reverent, constrained to win the world and lay it humbly at *her* feet; to reverence truth and to scorn with scorn unutterable all the thousand and one manifestations of the lie; to be loyal to king and country and God; to be gentle, courteous, kind to all life from highest to lowest; to stand face-front to the oncoming forces of evil and in that fight grimly to conquer or die: there is nothing nobler.

And yet not for all the glory of Don John, ideal Christian knight and hero of Lepanto, would I have one little stain of human blood on my white hands.

"New occasions teach new duties;
Time makes ancient good uncouth."

— *Lowell.*

Nevertheless he who would sympathetically and justly depict the past should be capable of entering into and all round estimating that ancient good now grown uncouth. And whatever the best men of any given age or time or clime unanimously hold as best must, in the deep heart of things, be best for that age or time or clime. The knight, the hero, the Crusader, the victor over the Saracens seemed best to the best men of the Middle Age.

Pope Pius V. earnestly advocated the cause of Venice. He appealed to the Christian monarchs of Europe to join with the Holy See in a League having for its object the total overthrow of the Ottoman empire. He urged the aggressive policy of the Turks under Solyman the Magnificent and his unworthy son and successor Selim II.; he vividly portrayed the atrocities of Turkish conquest and the blight upon civilization that ever unerringly followed in the wake of the Crescent; and he endeavored by all means in his power to arouse in the hearts of the children of the Church the spirit that had made possible the First Crusade.

All Europe at this time mourned its Christian captives who were languishing in Turkish dungeons or wasting away as galley slaves. Twelve thousand of these Christian captives were chained to the oars as galley slaves on the Moslem ships while the fight Lepanto was raging; their liberation and restoration to freedom formed the purest joy-pearl in the gem casket of that joyous victory.

Cyprus had just fallen into the hands of the Turks amid scenes of unparalleled barbarity: and against the Turk as the destroyer of civilization and the menace of Christendom all eyes were directed, all hearts beat with desire to avenge, slay, destroy: and all these feelings found outlet, and culmination and gratification in the battle of Lepanto, under Don John of Austria, the Christian knight.

OCEAN ENCOUNTERS.

Ocean instability, ocean vastness, ocean majestic indifference to the pigmy life and death struggles of men throw a magnetic glow over sea fights.

When the bay of Salamis changed gradually from greenish gray to red; when the Ionian sea slowly purpled off Actium, crimsoning the frightened barge of Cleopatra and of love maddened Anthony; when the waters at the entrance of the gulf Lepanto grew blood-red fed by trickling streams from five hundred galleys: did ocean care? The Titanic sinks and the billows dash high in foam play, they descend sportively with her into her grave hole, they arise and roll on: the Volturno blazes on a background of black sky, a foreground of flame-lit angry rolling waves: and does ocean care?

Don John arranged his battle line in a semi-circular stretch of about one mile embracing the entrance to the gulf of Lepanto (now Gulf Corinth). The Turkish fleet lay concealed somewhere on the water of the gulf and must come out at the entrance and fight openly or remain bottled up in the gulf until forced out by starvation. Don John knew his adversary, Ali Pasha, too well to dream that the latter alternative would be accepted by the sturdy Moslem.

Early Sunday morning (Oct. 7, 1571) Don John sighted a line of ships far in the gulf but making steadily for the opening. Battle was at hand. Don John, in his flagship, the Real, passed from vessel to vessel encouraging and animating his soldiers. "You have come," he said, "to fight the battle of the Cross; to conquer or to die. But whether you are to die or conquer, do your duty this day and you will secure a glorious immortality." He then returned to his position in the center of the semi-circle, and in that conspicuous position seen by all, he knelt in prayer under the far floating banner of the League. His example was followed by all, and the priests of whom there was at least one if not more on each galley, went around giving the last absolution to the men as they knelt in prayer.

The Ottoman shouts now filled the air as the long line of three hundred galleys arranged as a crescent, paused for a moment at the opening of the gulf. The center of the Christian fleet following Don John advanced to the Ottoman center commanded by Ali Pasha; the left wing under Barbarigo, the Venetian admiral, sought as adversary the opposing wing under Mahomet Sirocco; the right wing under Andrew Doria grappled with the opposing Mohammedan left under Ulrich Ali, dey of Algiers. For four hours the battle raged. So dense was the canopy of smoke enveloping the combatants that neither side knew for a certainty which was winning until the drawing down of the Ottoman banner and the hasty hauling up of the Banner of the League on board the flagship of Ali Pasha made known the result decisively. Shouts then rent the air and groans.

The Moslem left wing under the brave sea captain Ulrich Ali was engaged in a fierce grappling fight with Doria, and the advantage seemed to be with the Moslems. Don John seeing this, hastened to Doria's aid. Ulrich Ali, seeing that all was lost, ordered his men at the oars to make all possible speed for escape round the promontory. The Christian vessels gave chase, but the Moslem galleys sped with the speed of the wind and were soon lost to sight. About forty vessels were thus saved out of the three hundred that had taken part in the engagement. Of these one hundred and thirty were seized as prizes by the Christian forces, the rest having been sunk or burned in the fight.

The Ottoman loss is estimated between twenty-five thousand and thirty thousand; that of the Christians at eight thousand. The superior marksmanship of the allies and their use exclusively of firearms, while the Turks used in part bows and arrows; the better make and equipment of the Christian galleys—are among the causes to which human reason may attribute the incredible disparity between the Turkish loss and that of the Christians in this engagement. But there are many circumstances peculiar to this battle for which human reason can assign no cause.

It is related on good authority that as the Christian soldiers arose from prayer the wind which had hitherto been blowing steadily from the gulf, suddenly veered around and blew right into the faces of the enemy. In the course of the engagement the sun, too, reached the point where its rays shot into the eyes of the Turkish marksmen and caused them to err in their aim. Pope Pius V. who, while the battle was in progress, was closeted in consultation with a number of cardinals, in the Vatican, suddenly arose from his seat and approaching the window and casting up his eyes to the heavens exclaimed as tears of joy rolled down his cheeks, "A truce to business; our great task at present is to thank God for the victory He has just given the Christians."

DEATH OF ALI PASHA.

The struggle between The Real, Don John's flagship, and the galley bearing Ali Pasha was of course pivotal. Each commander felt that upon him and his ship depended the issue of the combat. Both were brave men, both must conquer or die: Don John conquered, Ali Pasha died.

The ships had grappled and a hand to hand conflict was raging upon the decks. Blood slowly trickled down the sides of the galleys and the waters were incarnadined.

In the heat of the engagement a musket ball struck the head of the Moslem commander. He fell prone and lay for some time unconscious upon a heap of the dying and the dead. But suddenly regaining consciousness he attempted to rise and was at once recognized by the surrounding Spanish soldiers. They were about to despatch him with their swords when the wily Moslem appealing to their natural cupidity made known to them the secret hiding place of his ship's treasure. The lure of gold led the soldiers to hasten below leaving their victim to chance life or death on the deck. But just as dear life seemed secured from the ruthless thrust of death, the wounded commander was confronted by a strangely savage figure with uplifted sword. It was one of the Christian galley slaves long chained on Ali's vessel and but that hour given freedom from the hated oar. In vain did Ali Pasha appeal to this soldier's cupidity; nothing seemed quite so desirable to him as the death of the man who had so long chained him a galley slave. The threatening sword fell unerringly upon the wounded Moslem chief and buried itself in his heart. With this retributive blow the tide of victory turned decisively in favor of the Christians.

DON JOHN OF AUSTRIA.

There are few characters upon the historic page more full in promise and yet futile in attainment than Don John of Austria. The idol of all Europe, the knight *sans peur et sans reproche*, the hero of Lepanto—at the age of twenty-four; he died seven years later in comparative obscurity; a rude hut hastily erected to receive the dying commander served as his last resting place upon earth.

As Don John lay in the agony of death, a terrific storm suddenly broke over the camp; and as in the case of Napoleon under somewhat similar circumstances, Don John partly arose, muttered incoherently of battle and victory, then sank back and died. Did the rattle of the storm suggest the din of battle? Or did vague visions of another storm arise associatively in memory? History relates that tho' that battle Sunday, Oct. 7, 1571, was a day of ideal autumn brightness, yet when the strife was fairly over and the battered galleys with their dead and wounded and sorely wearied men were heavily entering port, a storm suddenly arose: the skies darkened ominously, lightning flashed from the lowering clouds, thunder reverberated, and torrential rains poured down. For twenty-four hours the storm continued. Was nature indignantly weeping over the errors and sufferings of her children? Was she striving to wash out from old ocean—the rugged, primal, favorite work of her hands—those awful stains of blood?

As Don John had hastened to port under the gathering storm he gave orders that the Moslem galleys rendered worthless by the battle should be stripped of everything of value and then set on fire. And so it was that when safe in port the Christian conquerors looking out thro' the storm saw the burning ships. They luridly lit up the darkness and blazed wildly down to the waves—mutely eloquent witnesses of the horror and desolation of war.

Did the dulling senses of the hero of Lepanto see that scene, hear that storm—as the winds raged round his temporary shelter and death in blasting splendor closed over all? Or did the fair "castles in Spain" rise again spectrally with light upon them from beyond the grave as the dreamer of royal dreams sank down to the real? That wonderful African empire so near, so far: that beauteous bride, Mary Queen of Scots, liberated, released, restored by his own good sword; wooed and won and with her the throne of that imperious usurper Elizabeth Tudor: that smile of pontiffs, that commendation of Catholic Europe, that proud praise from the lips of his father's son, Philip II. of Spain—as he, the hero of Lepanto, the champion of Christendom, returned fresh-laureled from new combats and victories, a king, a crowned lover, an Emperor—Dreams!

> "Take, fortune, whatever you choose
> You gave and may take again;
> I've nothing 'twould pain me to lose,
> For I own no more castles in Spain."

Don John is buried in the Escorial. His name and fame are inseparably associated with the decisive victory of the Cross over the Crescent off the entrance to the gulf Lepanto.

An admirable painting of this battle *The Victory of the League* by Titian still adorns the walls of the Museo, Madrid.

The petition *Mary, Help of Christians* inserted on this occasion in the litany of Loretto bears evidence even today of the gratitude felt by Pius V. and with him all

Christendom for deliverance from the unspeakable Turk.

The historian Ranke speaking of the effects of this battle says: "The Turks lost all their old confidence after the battle of Lepanto. They had no equal to oppose to Don John of Austria. The day of Lepanto broke down the Ottoman supremacy."

CHAPTER XI.
THE INVINCIBLE ARMADA

Spain's proudly invincible Armada left Lisbon, May 20, 1588 with one hundred and forty ships and thirty thousand four hundred and ninety-seven men; fifty-three shattered vessels, and ten thousand men, vincible and humbled, returned to port Santander, Sept. 13, 1588. This disaster led to the decadence of Spain as a maritime power, and indirectly to the decline of Spanish dominance both in the old and in the new world.

The effects of any great event are not immediately discernible nor are its causes ever fully revealed. When Philip II. of Spain received with courteous equanimity his defeated admiral, the Duke of Medina Sidonia, and to his words,

> "And you see here, great King,
> All that remains of the Armada's might
> And of the flower of Spain."

made answer,

> "God rules above us!
> I sent you to contend with men and not
> With rocks and storms. You're welcome to Madrid."
>
> —*Schiller.*

did the great King see then either the causes or the consequences of the vincibility of his Invincible Armada!

The character of Philip II. is portrayed upon the historic page in colors of sharp contrast. To the Spaniards he was their Solomon, their "prudent king"; to Motley and the Netherlands he was "the demon of the South."

Philip II. was the finished product of his age and nation. Pride, intolerance, absolutism combined with excellent administrative ability, deep tho' narrow religious convictions, and rigorous sincerity, characterized both the man and the monarch. To a victim of an Auto da Fe he said with stern truthfulness, "If my own son were guilty like you I should lead him with my own hands to the stake."

As to Philip's really having delivered his son, Don Carlos, into the hands of the Grand Inquisitor as tragically told in Schiller's "Don Carlos", well that is drama, not history. But when a noted name and its suggested personality—for good or for evil and unfortunately less frequently for good than for evil—are once fascinatingly fixed in drama or story or song, not all the tomes of contradictory ev-

THE INVINCIBLE ARMADA

idence, not all the living archives of dead centuries, not Truth itself, can shatter the crystal charm or make it cease shining. Alexander the Great, world conqueror; Socrates, the Wise; Plato, poet-philosopher; Aristotle, master of them that know; Julius Cæsar, deplored of all nations; Mark Anthony, Cleopatra's lover; Nero, monster; Caligula-Commodus-Heliogabalus, crowned madmen; Marcus Aurelius, Emperor-philosopher; Charlemagne, the Good; Louis IX., the Saint; Louis XI., hypocrite; John of England, child murderer; Richard III., deformed devil; Henry VIII., wife-killer; Machiavelli, serpent-sophist; Louis XIV., despot, *Arbiter Elegantiarum*; Elizabeth, Good Queen Bess; Mary, Queen of Scots, the lovely unfortunate; Philip II. of Spain, bigot: thus are they fixed in the charmed circle of literature and thus shall they glitter forever.

Is history itself any more reliable than drama? As to facts, Yes; as to motives, intentions, cumulative causes, results, all round truth, No. "Histories are as perfect as the historian is wise, and is gifted with an eye and a soul," says the astute Carlyle; and every honest author feels at deepest heart the truth of these words. The soft art of omission is known to every artist of the pen. And condemnation euphemistically balanced by excusing comment may, in one artistic sentence, satisfy at once a writer's conscience, his subjectivity, and the claims of his peculiar environment. Can any one doubt that it was thus Macaulay wrote his brilliant history of England? And even granted almost the impossible—that an historian be ruggedly truthful and fearlessly sincere; he is not thereby rendered wise, nor is he necessarily gifted with an eye and a soul.

So in colors of sharp contrast upon the historic page will Philip II. ever be portrayed; but both can't be right. Perhaps tho' they may be as sundered extremes of a prismatic ray which, when complementary coloring shall have been added, will become white light.

STORMS.

Truly it was against storms and rocks as well as against such rough sea-dogs as Drake and Hawkins and Raleigh and Frobisher and Howard that the Invincible Armada contended. In the beginning of the northward cruise as the Armada was rounding the corner of Spain, off Corunna, a violent tempest arose. The frail caravels, and galleons and galleasses of 1588 were not so independent of wave and wind as are the Dreadnoughts of 1914. Yet ocean is still master of man; and man's most titan-like Titanic is but a puny plaything in old Neptune's hand.

Several vessels were lost in the storm, and the fleet was so badly damaged that in consequence the Spanish Admiral was obliged to stop off at Corunna for repairs. July 12th, after so inauspicious a beginning, the fleet was again on its way northward.

Alexander Farnese, Prince of Parma, captain general of all the Spanish armies, was at Dunkirk with a flotilla of large flat-bottomed barges awaiting the Armada to convoy him and his army across the channel. His plan was to invade England by way of the Thames and land his veteran forces in London.

"Alexander Farnese, prince of Parma, captain general of the Spanish armies, and governor of the Spanish possessions in the Netherlands, was beyond all comparison the greatest military genius of his age. He was also highly distinguished for political wisdom and sagacity, and for his great administrative talents. He was idolized by his troops, whose affection he knew how to win without relaxing their discipline or diminishing his own authority. Pre-eminently cool and circumspect in his plans, but swift and energetic when the moment arrived for striking a decisive blow, neglecting no risk that caution could provide against, conciliating even the populations of the districts which he attacked by his scrupulous good faith; his moderation, and his address; Farnese was one of the most formidable generals that ever could be placed at the head of an army designed not only to win battles, but to effect conquests. Happy it is for England and the world that this island was saved from becoming an arena for the exhibition of his powers." Creasy.

As in 1588 Alexander Farnese with a chosen army awaited at Dunkirk the assistance of the Armada both to clear the seas of Dutch and English war ships and to convoy in safety his flotilla to the coast of England: so, too, in 1805 Napoleon Bonaparte awaited at Boulogne for Villeneuve to do him a like service; and in both cases the English fleet took the offensive and destroyed at one blow both the protective war boats of the enemy and the hopeful plans of the man who waited. The sea fights at Calais Roads and at Trafalgar are perhaps negatively momentous in history but not the less momentous.

The Spanish fleet after some disastrous fighting with the English cruisers off the coast of Plymouth succeeded in reaching Calais Roads (July 27). Here they were quickly semi-circled by the combined Dutch and English fleet under Lord Charles Howard, high admiral of England. The Spanish ships were far greater in bulk than those of the opposing force and in the harbor of Calais they were huddled together "like strong castles fearing no assault, the lesser placed in the middle ward." The lighter English ships, no longer able to use their two best assets, nimbleness and advantage of the wind, clung doggedly around these ocean leviathans awaiting the hour of opportunity. At length early on the morning of the 29th the English Admiral succeeded in thrusting eight Greek fire-ships in among the compact wooden war vessels. The effect was electrical. The Spanish ships cut their cables and were dispersed and the fight ship to ship was soon in full progress. All day long from early dawn till dark this battle raged. The Spaniards were driven out from Calais Roads and past the Flemish ports and far out beyond Dunkirk where the Prince of Parma waited. The English then ceased pursuit. Lord Henry Seymour with an able squadron was left to maintain the blockade of the Flemish port and to render ineffectual the activities of the Prince of Parma.

Northward sped the vincible Armada farther and farther from sunny Spain. She had many wounded men on board ships, her provisions were failing, the channel filled with victorious Dutch and English war boats offered no hope of a way of return, and at last in desperation the Spanish admiral directed the course of his ships around the northern coast of Scotland and Ireland. What a long and cruel way home for wounded soldiers, starving sailors, and disheartened generals! But even here ill luck pursued them. A storm arose as they were passing thro' the Orkneys; their vessels were dispersed, many were lost. About thirty ships were afterwards wrecked on the west coast of Ireland, and those of the crews who succeeded in reaching the shore were immediately put to death. It is estimated that fourteen thousand thus perished.

And in September of that memorable year there came straggling ship by ship into the port Santander all that were left of the gallant fleet that had sailed away five months ago to subdue England and so win all Europe for Spain.

Nor was that plan at all chimerical, nor its realization improbable. Spain was at that time in possession of Portugal, Naples, Sicily, Milan, Franche-Compte, and the Netherlands; in Africa she controlled Tunis, Oran, the Cape Verde and the Canary islands; in Asia, the Philippine and Sunda Islands and part of the Moluccas; in the New World, the empire of Peru, and of Mexico, New Spain, Chili, Hispaniola and Cuba. Only England held out against the power of Spain and stood adamantine to all her threats, cajolery, caresses. Only England stood between Philip II. of Spain and Spanish dominance in the old and in the New World. English buccaneers seized upon his galleons on their return gem-laden from Peru and Mexico. Drake the "master robber of the New World" had signally dishonored Philip of Spain and had in requital been honored by the English queen with the title *Sir Francis*. England must be destroyed (Britannia delenda est.) Spain seemed powerful enough by land and by sea to be as a new Rome to old Carthage: but winds and waves and rocky coasts and adamantine Englishmen reversed the Roman story (Britannia non deleta est.)

THE SIXTEENTH CENTURY.

"What we *appear* is subject to the judgment
Of all mankind; and what we *are*, of no man."

Schiller in "Mary Stuart."

These lines upon the lips of Elizabeth Tudor are her condemnation in the judgment of all mankind. Short sighted, indeed, and headed directly towards the rapids of the all revealing Real is the mortal who thus honors appearances.

Elizabeth would have Mary Stuart put to death, but would *seem* to have tried to save her: Elizabeth would sign the death warrant, but would *seem* to have been constrained, to have done so regretfully, to have recalled the fatal sentence when, alas! too late. But all this flimsy Seeming has been blown away by the rugged years; and that which this Machiavellian queen thought subject to the judgment of no man has become her condemnation in the eyes of all.

So close they lie together now in old Westminster Abbey—these rival queens who once so cordially feared and hated one another! and for whose conflicting ambitions all Britain was not room enough, but one must die! How ignoble seems now the strife, how despicable the deed of culminant hate, how diaphanous all the Seeming! Was it worth while?

The death of Mary, Queen of Scots, at the hands of her cousin Queen Elizabeth aroused a feeling of angry indignation in every court of Europe. France, Spain, and the Vatican, openly denounced the deed. And it was, in great measure, in execration of this unnatural cruelty that Pope Sextus V. espoused the cause of Philip II. of Spain and urged and aided the invasion of England.

Strange that such men as Edmund Spenser, author of *Færie Queen* and Sir Walter Raleigh, mirror of chivalry, should have been among the foremost to demand the death of the Scottish queen. But those were turbulent times. Life and death never played the mortal game more boldly and recklessly and desperately than in the sixteenth century. The magic of the New World was upon the old; the glamour of gem-lit El Dorados shimmered across the seas; and thither responsively rushed in shaky ships and leaky caravels those whom the gods would destroy made mad by the bite of the gold-tarantula. "We are as near to heaven by sea as by land", shouted Sir Humphrey Gilbert as his frail bark was lost in the storm; as his deck lights rose high and dashed low and darkened far down 'neath the sea-lashing storm.

And night with wondering stars looked down upon De Soto's lordly grave. And then as now and even throughout the historic ages, the prehistoric, the geologic—the thundering waters fell and formed Niagara Falls. In silvery moonlight, in dazzling sun-radiance rainbow-frilled, in blinding white of winter, in rainy spring, in saber flashing summer storm—the thunder-waters fell; they fall; they shall fall.

When Columbus and his crew, secretly fearful of falling off the good old planet Earth, sailed the unknown sea; while Cortes conquered Mexico (not yet calm); while Pizarro ravaged Peru; while Balboa ascended the Andean heights and "silent upon a peak in Darien" first saw the vast Pacific; while De Soto died and was buried; while Drake circumnavigated the globe; while Mary, Queen of Scots laid her head on the block and the axe fell; while the Invincible Armada hurrying northward away from the foe, sailed brokenly back to Spain by way of the Orkneys: while Julius Cæsar fell pierced with twenty-three wounds; while Hannibal crossed the Alps; while Alexander, world-conqueror, aged thirty-two died at old Babylon; while Pericles of Athens reigned imperishably; while Sardis burned and Sardis was avenged; while Marathon, Salamis, Thermopylæ, Platæa, Mycale were fighting; while Babylon the Great was captured by Cyrus; while the Memphian pyramids were building; while the great Sphinx of Gizeh rose solemnly; while griffins and dragons and gummy pterodactyls winged the air; while plesiosauri and ichthyosauri fought for the empire of ocean; while the original of the Pittsburgh Diplodocus Carnegiei was sixty feet somewhere—why, even then were the waters rolling over the rock now called Niagara; even then Niagara Falls that fall and shall fall were falling.

SEA FIGHTS.

The hostile encounters by land throughout the historic ages have been practically countless; sea fights are few. Man feels intuitively that the yielding wave is not the fit place for battle. Salamis, Actium, Lepanto, Calais Roads are the chief naval engagements of history.

When Rome had won her first game in world conquest and all Italy was Rome,

THE INVINCIBLE ARMADA

Carthage was mistress of the Mediterranean, and without her permission no man might even wash his hands in her "Phœnician Lake." Triremes and quinqueremes with proudly curving prows scudded over the blue waters or huddled together in port as bevies of black swans.

And Rome had no fleet. But Rome could learn from her enemies; and when a wrecked Carthaginian galley was dashed against the Latian coast, Rome quickly learned the art of making galleys; and within two months the waving forest near the coast was metamorphosed into a fleet of one hundred and twenty Roman triremes.

And when the pain of growth was upon Rome making further conquest fatally necessary, she embarked unsteadily upon her late waving forest trees and went reeling forth to meet the swan bevies of the Mediterranean. The hostile fleets engaged and Rome's was annihilated.

Then these sullen young-world children wildly wept, as did Romulus and Remus, perhaps, in the cave of the she-wolf. But when they were suckled and made strong with the milk of defeat, these wild young Romans built themselves another fleet. And Duillius devised a grappling contrivance whereby to catch and hold the enemy's ship until a drawbridge could be thrown across o'er which the short-sword Roman soldiers might pass and so fight on the deck hand to hand as on land.

Again the hostile fleets engaged on the blue Mediterranean. But as the haughty quinqueremes with their decks filled with archers bore down upon the awkward Roman triremes, the grappling "hands" arose, the quinqueremes were grappled. Consternation prevailed among the Carthaginians as the drawbridges from ship to ship were thrown across, and the dreaded Roman soldiers short-sword in hand were seen slaughtering the archers and the rowers. Rome's first naval victory was won.

If the blue Mediterranean could make known all that has taken place upon its waves and shores—what a Homer of the waters it would be! But nature is indifferent to the human tragedy.

That other scene off the coast of Carthage, after the second Punic war, when Rome demanded as a condition of peace that the Carthaginian fleet should be destroyed—yet burns upon the historic page, but the waters that once reddened with the flames just ripple unrememberingly. Five hundred galleys—towering quinqueremes, sturdy triremes—were led out from the harbor before the mourning gaze of the dethroned Queen of the Seas, and set on fire; she watched them blaze down to the laughing waters.

Actium was fought on the Adriatic off the promontory on the west coast of Greece. Here half the world was bartered for one fleeing galley and one woman. While the conflict was yet doubtful and victory seemed even favorably inclined to perch upon the prow of Anthony's vessel, the barge of Cleopatra shudderingly backed out from the bloody fray, wavered, turned, and sped southward. Marc Anthony followed. Upon the defeat of the allied Roman and Egyptian forces at Actium and over the tragically dead forms of Anthony and Cleopatra, Octavius Cæsar arose to world dominance, becoming Augustus Cæsar, Emperor, Pater Patriæ, and one man Ruler of Rome, Mistress of the world.

Lepanto was fought at the entrance of the Gulf of Corinth, not far from Actium. Here the Cross triumphed over the Crescent and rescued Europe from the deadly blight of Islamism. Don John of Austria, aged twenty-four, led the Christian forces; Alexander Farnese (Prince of Parma), then a youth of twenty, won here his first of many laurels under the generously approving eyes of his young cousin-commander, Don John.

And seventeen years later (1571-1588) the Prince of Parma, Captain general of all the Spanish armies, awaited impatiently at Dunkirk for Admiral Medina Sidonia to clear the channel of hostile vessels so that he and his veteran army might sail across and attack old England. He watched the fight off Gravelines. How his hot Spanish heart must have indignantly throbbed even to bursting, as helplessly cooped in port with a flotilla of unarmed barges to protect, and Lord Seymour with a strong blockading squadron at the mouth of the harbor, he could only see and know and acutely feel that a fearful battle was raging all day long from dawn till dark and that Spain was losing—Spain had lost. One by one hurrying northward past the Flemish ports limped the disabled Spanish ships; English and Dutch cruisers followed in fierce pursuit.

The invasion of England by way of the Thames, the conquest of an inveterate foe, Success proudly placing a flaming carbuncle upon the coronet of the Prince of Parma, the approving glance of Philip and of the fair girl-queen Isabella, Spanish dominance in the old and in the new world—all as burst bubbles died down in gray mist as twilight descended, as dark night gathered over the wave and the world and the fleeing scattered shattered ships of Spain's vincible Armada.

CHAPTER XII.
NASEBY

The battle of Naseby was, perhaps, the anticipative preventive of an English "French Revolution." The difference between Cromwell's Ironsides and the gay Frondeurs measures the difference between the English people and the French.

Charles I. aimed to be in England what Louis XIV. was in France. Both fully believed in the divine right of Kings; both quoted as their favorite text of Scripture, "Where the word of a King is there is power; and who may say unto him 'What doest thou?'" But Louis dealt with the fickle Frondeurs and Charles with Cromwell's Ironsides; and this racial difference had as divergent results — absolutism for Louis le Grand and the block for Charles Stuart.

There will always be difference of opinion as to Cromwell's place in history. Was he liberator or tyrant, Christian ruler or barbarously fanatic despot? There can be but one opinion as to the injustice of the trial, condemnation, and death of Charles. The Rump Parliament was certainly not representative of England. It was Cromwell's creature as arbitrarily as ever the Star Chamber was Charles'.

"Must crimes be punished but by other crimes, and greater criminals?" — Byron.

But as a force in favor of constitutional government and civic liberty, however abused in immediate practice; and as a threatening protest against the abuse of power in high places; and as a veiled challenge of defiance to every absolute monarch — the battle fought June 14, 1645, at Naseby, Northamptonshire, between the Royalists under Charles I. and the Parliamentarians under Fairfax must ever be considered a victory decisive and for all time advantageous.

QUEEN HENRIETTA MARIA.

Henrietta Maria was the daughter of Henry IV. of France, the first Bourbon, and his second wife, Maria de Medici. At the age of fifteen she was married to Charles I. of England; and her best and happiest years as wife, mother, and Queen were spent in England.

In this princess many of the leading Italian, French and English characteristics were met and happily blended. Her dark, lithe beauty (as shown in her portrait by Van Dyke), her musical ability, instrumental and vocal, her fiery-hearted fidelity to the religion of her mother, were, perhaps, her heritage from sunny Italy; the France of Richelieu might, as an environment, conduce favorably to that diplomatic waywardness which, in early years, invariably won for the sweet girl-wife whatsoever her heart might desire; but perhaps from England, land of realism, chilly fogs, and Cromwellian barbarity, she imbibed her sturdy spirit of fortitude and heroic endurance of sorrow.

"To bear is to conquer our fate", and to refuse to bear and to apparently end all by self-destruction, is to fail to conquer our fate.

The hopes and promises of religion are of inestimable value as an aid in the endurance of sorrows. When the dread culmination of all earthly fears and horrors—the beheading of Charles I.—clashed full upon the widowed heart of Queen Henrietta Maria, she withdrew at once from the court of Paris and sought solace in seclusion and prayer. The convent, not the court; the divine, not the human; the hopes and promises of religion as red-glowed in the sanctuary of a Carmelite convent chapel, held the balm that soothed her wounded soul in that awful culminant woe.

Which is better—to bear or to fail to bear? to hope and endure or despair and die? to pray and bless God saying, *The Lord gave and the Lord has taken away, blessed be the name of the Lord*, or to wither away in cursing and impotent hate? to believe and grow strongly peaceful in the belief that God is good and all is for the best; that all is little and short that passes away with time; that God's explanation shall exultingly explain forever and ever—or to doubt, negative, deny, and bitterly live and despairingly die? Even as a matter of merely human wisdom, it is well to believe in the hopes and promises of religion.

The monastic sanctuaries that arise wherever the Catholic Church flourishes, and that lure into their prayerful solitudes the "hearts that are heavy with losses and weary with dragging the crosses too heavy for mortals to bear" are surely indicative of a far higher and happier state of society than that whose godless defiance finds suicidal expression in the insidious drug, the deadly acid, the desperate bullet.

The houses of Euthanasia of the near Socialistic future are surely as stones unto bread in comparison with the monastic sanctuaries of the Middle Ages.

WONDERS OF PORTRAITS.

How wonderful is the art which can impress upon canvas and so preserve from generation to generation and from century to century, a lifelike presentment of men and women whose flesh and blood realities have long since mouldered dust with dust! The canvas endures; the man dies?—Ah, no! he has but shuffled off the earth-garment and left it earth with earth; he lives.

The Van Dyke portraits of Queen Henrietta Maria, Charles I. and the children of Charles I. are mutely eloquent. The well-known picture, "Baby Stuart", a detail from the group, "Children of Charles I." suggests the high tide of love and happiness in the life of Queen Henrietta Maria. She was then surrounded by everything that heart could desire,—wealth, honor, power, a husband's unbounded love and confidence and three beautiful and most promising children. They were Mary, who later married William, Prince of Orange; Charles, who, at the Restoration, became the "Merry Monarch" of England, and James, the baby Stuart, who later became the unfortunate James II., the monarch who lost his crown, and whose daughter Mary, wedded to her cousin, William, Prince of Orange, son of that sister Mary, who, in the portrait, stands at his side, abetted the deposition of her father and wore his crown.

There is something eloquently pathetic in the portraits of men and women who have fallen victims to a tragic fate. The principle of contrast is, doubtless, here at work, setting side by side with the hour of portrayal that other hour of bitter death. Marie Antoinette and her children, as fixed upon canvas by the court painter, Madame Vigee LeBrun, derive their rich tonal qualities—warm grays and reds, their charm of evanescence, their magically somber fascination, from the shadows of the Conciergerie and the guillotine.

The portrait of Charles I. as painted by Van Dyke, must ever suggest to the thoughtful student of history that scene, disgraceful alike to the English nation and to human nature which took place on the scaffold just outside Whitehall Palace.

Yes; there are two sides to every question, and one is a ruler exercising arbitrary power and impregnated with belief in the divine right of kings and claiming it his prerogative to break up his parliament and govern alone; the other is an assembly of men, nominally a parliament, so narrowly fanatic and steeped in human hate that they demanded as condition under which they would agree to levy taxes for Charles I. to use in aid of Protestant Holland, that he should first order every Catholic priest in his own realm to be put to death and the property of all Catholics to be confiscated. Charles refused. This side of the cause of the rupture between Charles I. and his Parliament has not the historic prominence of the other side. Why? Not very hard to tell *why* if one considers attentively the writers of the history of that period.

"I hope to meet my end with calmness. Do not let us speak of the men into whose hands I have fallen. They thirst for my blood, they shall have it. God's will be done, I give Him thanks. I forgive them all sincerely, but let us say no more about them"—these words addressed to Bishop Juxon by Charles a few days before his death attest the inherent nobility of his nature. Whatever the life of Charles I. may have been, his death was kingly; and if death is the echo of life then, too, his life must have been vocal with virtues. But what virtue can outshine or even illumine the black chaos of creed-fanaticism, odium, obloquy? What power can break up and restore to their original settings the half-truths, untruths, errors and lies glitteringly crystalized in history, drama, story and song? Does time right ancient wrongs, readjust and make-whole torn, century-scattered truths? We dream so; we say so; but at deepest heart we whisper *No*.

With unruffled calmness, with dignity, with kingly grace, Charles I. stepped from the opening of what had been in happier days his banqueting hall and advanced upon the scaffold. In the words of Agnes Strickland:

"It was past 1 o'clock before the grisly attendants and apparatus of the scaffold were ready. Colonel Hacker led the king through his former banqueting hall, one of the windows of which had originally been contrived to support stands for public pageantries; it had been taken out and led to the platform raised in the street. The noble bearing of the King as he stepped on the scaffold, his beaming eyes and high expression, were noticed by all who saw him. He looked on all sides for his people, but dense masses of soldiery only presented themselves far and near. He was out of hearing of any persons but Juxon and Herbert, save those who were interested in his destruction. The soldiers preserved a dead silence; this time they did not insult him. The distant populace wept, and occasionally raised mournful cries in blessings and prayers for him. The king uttered a short speech, to point out that every institute of the original constitution of England had been subverted with the sovereign power. While he was speaking someone touched the axe, which was laid enveloped in black crepe on the block. The king turned round hastily and exclaimed, 'Have a care of the axe. If the edge is spoiled it will be the worse for me.'

"The king put up his flowing hair under a cap; then, turning to the executor asked, 'Is any of my hair in the way?' 'I beg your majesty to push it more under your cap,' replied the man, bowing. The bishop assisted his royal master to do so and observed to him: 'There is but one stage more, which, though turbulent and troublesome, is yet a very short one. Consider, it will carry you a great way—even from earth to heaven.' 'I go,' replied the king, 'from a corruptible to an incorruptible crown.'

"He unfastened his cloak and took off the medallion of the order of the Garter. The latter he gave to Juxon, saying with emphasis, 'Remember!' Beneath the medallion of St. George was a secret spring which removed a plate ornamented with lilies, under which was a beautiful miniature of his Henrietta. The warning word, which has caused many historical surmises, evidently referred to the fact that he only had parted with the portrait of his beloved wife at the last moment of his existence. He then took off his coat and put on his cloak, and pointing to the block, said to the executioner: 'Place it so that it will not shake.' 'It is firm, sir,' replied the man. 'I shall say a short prayer,' said the king, 'and when I hold out my hand thus, strike.' The king stood in profound meditation, said a few words to himself, looked upward on the heavens, then knelt and laid his head on the block. In about a minute he stretched out his hands, and his head was severed at one blow."

SORROW.

News travelled slowly in the days of long ago; and the trial, death and burial of Charles I. were over long before intelligence of the dire happenings in England had been carried into France. Queen Henrietta Maria, then in the Louvre Palace, Paris, had just received into her motherly arms her second son, James, who had successfully passed through the belligerent lines and reached safety in Paris. This joy was soon dulled into woe.

Ominous whispers among the Louvre circle and pitying glances caused the queen to make inquiries. The worst was soon told. The queen had expected imprisonment, perhaps even deposition and exile, but death, the official beheading of an

NASEBY 73

English sovereign—had not once entered into her mind as among the possibilities. The queen sat silent and tearless among her sympathizing English attendants. Pere Gamache approached. She received him apathetically. Her aunt, the Duchess de Vendome, took her hand and held it caressingly—but the Queen seemed in a state of frozen woe; no moan, no sigh, no tear. Pere Gamache withdrew unobserved and searching through the royal chambers he found the little Princess Henriette, the four-year-old idol of the once happy Stuart home. Leading the child gently by the hand, he returned to the scene of grief.

At the touch of baby hands, the impress of childish kisses, the unhappy Queen seemed slowly to come back to life even as it was, and clasping her little daughter in rapturous tenderness to her breast she wept. Long and wildly she wept and the frightened child weeping responsively and clinging helplessly to her bosom saved her at last to sanity and to heroic endurance.

Tennyson has beautifully expressed this power of childish love and helplessness to save a mother from despair:

> Home they brought her warrior dead;
> She nor swoon'd, nor utter'd cry,
> All her maidens, watching said,
> "She must weep or she will die."
>
> Then they praised him, soft and low,
> Called him worthy to be loved,
> Truest friend and noblest foe;
> Yet she neither spoke nor moved.
>
> Stole a maiden from her place,
> Lightly to the warrior stept
> Took the face-cloth from his face;
> Yet she neither moved nor wept.
>
> Rose a nurse of ninety years,
> Set his child upon her knee—
> Like summer tempest came her tears—
> "Sweet my child, I live for thee."

A few days later the Queen withdrew from the French court for a brief period of retirement and prayer in the Carmelite Convent.

MILTON.

While the drama in high places was playing before the world, a more enduring side scene was enacting in a quiet English home. John Milton, in political disgrace, in sorrow of soul, and in total blindness was dictating to his daughters the lines of "Paradise Lost." Cromwell and his Roundheads, the Merry Monarch and his dissolute court, James II. and his sorrows, passed away; the visions seen by the blind old bard remain.

As literary immortality is the highest prize that fate holds for mortals it is fitting that the cost of attainment should be proportionately high. And in this adjustment fate is inexorable. Heart's blood and tears wrought into a book give it enduring qualities: much, much; little, little; some, some; none, none. The dictum of Horace in the olden day, *Si vis me flere*, etc., is still the exponent of an author's power.

That poem by Mrs. Browning, "A Musical Instrument," has fixed in rainbow evanescence—a Thoughts' Niagara Bridal Veil—ten thousand blending, blinding truths and beauties that prose could never hold or catch.

Is the prize worth the price? In itself, No; but in the soul-growth that its mastery implies and in the soul-wealth that it makes one's own forever and ever, Yes. Then, too, they to whom Fame shines as an ever luring star, urging on, on, incessantly even through blood and tears, are so formed by their fate that the prize seems to them worth while; its winning seems life's only good, its loss, life's supreme sorrow. "The attractions are proportional to the destinies."

So who shall judge his unknown neighbor? Who shall justly say, *Thou fool* to the man who must needs follow his fate? Who shall justly pity him whose poverty, disgrace, bitterness of heart, and blindness of soul and body—lead to the star-luring heights of literary immortality?

Milton was Latin secretary under Oliver Cromwell and a man of great influence at the court. He shared in the amnesty proclaimed by Charles II. at the Restoration. Milton's remaining years were spent in retirement and literary labors.

The return of the Stuarts shattered all his hopes, religious and political. He seemed to see in the Stuart restoration the first gathering gloom of a darkness which should overwhelm himself, England, and all the earth. Subjectively this was true. Milton never saw beyond that gathering cloud; and when the culminant blackness of his own blindness closed in upon him, then, too, into a common gloom sank Milton, England and all the earth.

> "And darkness shows us worlds by night
> We never see by day."

Would Paradise Lost have been born into literature if Milton had not become blind?

Would we of today find congenial that Milton of the old Puritanical day? Do we admire the Miltonic God? Milton liked best his Lucifer, and that liking elusively throbs through Paradise Lost and elicits response.

CHARLES II.

There must have been a great measure of compensation to Charles I. in the filial devotion of his household. It is related that Prince Charles, eldest son, and heir apparent to the throne, sent to his father, when in prison, a document *carte blanche* signed with his name. And in a letter enclosed the Prince assured his father that whatever conditions he should see fit to make with Cromwell and his followers relative to the succession would be agreeable to him, in token whereof he had signed his name to the document. There was something heroic in that, and something even more magnanimously heroic in the response of Charles I. He at once tore the document to pieces, fearing that the enemy might get possession of it and make use of it against Prince Charles. He wrote tenderly to his son, admitting the pleasure his generous offer had given, but declaring that death would be preferable to any act whereby the rights of his children should be tampered with or signed away.

It is well to note these nobler actions and emotions in the lives of kings: the ambitious selfishness and cruelty of a Macbeth, a King John, a Richard III. are pedestaled for all the world to see; why not the mutual magnanimity of the Stuarts? Truly the evil that men do lives after them, the good is oftimes interred with their bones.

At the death of Cromwell, after a five years' stormy reign as Lord Protector of England, and after a twelve years' exile of the family of Charles I., the people of England unanimously welcomed the restoration of the Stuarts. Charles II.—known in France under this title since the death of Charles I.—was crowned King of England.

The times were troubled. Roundhead and Cavalier still stood at misunderstanding enmity one directly opposed to the other and never the twain might meet. The pendulum swung with bewildering rapidity from harshly somber Cromwellian Puritanism to the excessive dissipation of the Court of the Merry Monarch: the country followed the pendulum.

Charles II., while humane on the whole, and more inclined to ease and pleasure than to troublesome revenge, yet displayed a touch of the savage in his treatment of the body of Oliver Cromwell. He ordered that it be disinterred and the head struck off. This was done; and the ghastly head of the man who had ruled England with a rod of iron for five years, was fastened to the gibbet at Tyburn.

Horrible is the hate which pursues its victim beyond death and wreaks vengeance upon an unresisting mass of putrefaction! All such excesses, no matter by whom committed or under what provocation, are atavistic expressions of the jackal and the tiger in the heart of man.

Truly there is no eye that can foresee the future! Cromwell, passing for the thousandth time through the thoroughfare of Tyburn, saw not there his own head fastened to a gibbet. Charles I., at the stately banquet board of Whitehall Palace, saw not the great end window of the hall opening upon the scaffold. And we, secure in the hour, see not that other hour of fatal import that yet shall be; and—'tis well.

DEATH OF QUEEN HENRIETTA.

Queen Henrietta Maria was not present at the scenes of acclamation which welcomed the return of her son, Charles II. She was at that time happily absorbed in the forth-coming marriage of her charming daughter, the Princess Henriette Maria, to Philip, Duke of Orleans, brother of Louis XIV.

Some time later Queen Henrietta Maria went to England. She resided there three years, but her heart's best interests were in sunny France where her idolized daughter, the Duchess of Orleans, moved amid the gay court of Versailles as its chief honor and ornament. Charles II. and his wife, Catherine, of Braganza, reluctantly bade farewell to the Queen-mother after accompanying her as far as the Nore; but doubtless there was secret joy in the heart of Henrietta Maria as the foggy shores of England receded from view and France arose in expectancy.

Then, too, all seemed calm in England; Charles II. and his wife were high in popular favor. Her second son, James, Duke of York, was happily married and surrounded by a promising family. James' eldest daughter, the Lady Mary, later Queen Mary II. of England, was a great favorite with the affectionate grandmother, Henrietta Maria. Anne, James' second daughter, afterward Queen Anne of England, was also attached to the kindly old Queen-mother.

The old-age years of Henrietta Maria rolled on in comparative happiness. Some lives seem to have their sorrows scattered uniformly over the years, a gentle drizzle, never dazzling sunlight; other lives are marked by dynamic contrasts—brilliancy, ecstatic light suddenly blackened by tornado blasts and torn by lurid lightning, and after that, calm again and even the bright light.

Queen Henrietta Maria's tornado blast and searing lightning flash came full upon her when her husband was beheaded; her later years were calmly happy. In philanthropic labors, in the exercise of all the gentle charities of the Christian heart, in the hopeful fulfilment of religious obligations, the old age years drifted calmly to the great Calm.

It chanced that at that time the use of opium as a sedative, narcotic, and harmless medicine was in vogue at the court. M. Valot, favorite physician of Louis XIV., ordered it for the Queen. In the best of spirits and laughing at the supposed wonderful qualities of the new panacea, Henrietta Maria took the prescribed drug. An hour later she fell into a peaceful slumber; the night passed and the day passed, and still she slept. Alarm was felt, her son-in-law, the Duke of Orleans, was soon at her bedside; the little granddaughter, Anne, was brought near in hopes of arousing the dormant sensibilities—but in vain. Queen Henrietta had sunk into the calm; it was too good to leave; she stayed, sank deeper, deeper, and with a little sigh of relief she died.

BOSSUET'S SERMON.

Jacques Benigne Bossuet, the eloquent pulpit orator of the court of Louis XIV., added a classic to French literature in his masterly discourse at the obsequies of Henrietta Maria. It was delivered in the convent chapel of the nuns of the Visitation of Chaillot, whom the late Queen particularly favored, and for whom she had founded the convent.

The nobility of France were gathered together on this occasion, the "most illustrious assembly of the world" sat spell-bound under the eloquence of the "Eagle of Meaux." Bossuet had proved equal to his opportunity.

Perhaps, though, Bossuet is better known today by that other funeral oration delivered some months later at the obsequies of Queen Henrietta Maria's youngest daughter, Henriette of England, Duchess of Orleans.

When the old die, well—there can be no Shelleyan lamentation.

> "Grief made the young Spring wild,
> And she threw down her opening buds
> As if she autumn were and they dead leaves."
>
> *—Shelley.*

The young spring may, indeed, thus lavishly lament for the young, but not for the old. When a poet Keats, aged twenty-six, lies brokenheartedly and beautifully dead; when a queenly woman, wife and bereaved mother, aged twenty-eight, lies pathetically dead—oh, then, all that Shelley may poetically declare, all that Bossuet may magically proclaim, seem fitting and just and true. We understand the young Spring tantrums; and the sobbings of the buds as roughly sundered from the grief-swept trees, seem strangely familiar, as though ages ago we ourselves had thus wildly wept when the world was young.

Wealth, station, honor, health, happiness, youth, beauty, love—today; and the tomb tomorrow! This contrast has ever most forcefully appealed to the human heart. Bossuet knew full well the force of this appeal and again the orator and the occasion were well met.

"O vanity," he exclaimed, "O nothingness! O mortals, ignorant of their destiny! Ten months ago would she have believed it? And you, my hearers, would you have thought, while she was shedding so many tears in this place, while I was discharging a like office for the Queen, her mother—that she would so soon assemble you here to deplore her own loss? 'Vanity of vanities; all is vanity.' Nothing is left for me to say but that that is the only sentiment which, in presence of so strange a casualty, grief so well grounded and so poignant permits me to indulge. No; after what we have just seen, health is but a name, life is but a dream, glory is but a shadow, charms and pleasures are but a dangerous diversion."

REFLECTIONS.

"Keep cool, it will be all one in a hundred years." So we say to others, so we try to persuade ourselves; but the tempestuous teapot seems fatally fixed over the live coals of life and the teapot tempest must as fatally follow. So mightily important, so imperative, so irresistibly puissant where those seeming geyser-forces in their day; perhaps we who laugh at their spent spray would more wisely learn the lessons they may teach us.

But just as a matter of spent spray and evanishing iridescence, those struggles of the long ago seem magically beautiful; and the men and women who figured prominently in them seem to peer through the mist even as flame-light from which flame has fled, even as pictured pain, reflex sorrows, unrealities—spray-shrouded, color-clouded. Cleopatra, nobly dead, a Queen forever; ugly old Socrates growing humanly dear and beautiful to all the ages as he drinks the poison-hemlock; Marie Antoinette, in the tumbrel, at the guillotine, under the glittering blade; Charles I. upon the scaffold, on the block awaiting the headsman's blow—these things have been, but now they are not; yet they endure.

CHAPTER XIII.
BLENHEIM

Blenheim, Ramillies, Oudenarde, and Malplaquet—somehow these names lie contiguous in the mind; so stored away, perhaps, in the brain cells long ago, and thus forever associative.

Where is all that we know when it is not in play upon the plane of consciousness? Where is the music of a Rachmaninoff—while he sleeps? the reminiscent wealth of a Gladstone—while he plays with his great grandchild? the genius of an Edgar Allan Poe—while narcotic night silences the streets of Baltimore?

"Potentially down in subconsciousness," says my glib psychologist. Eloquent answer! But where and what *is* subconsciousness?

Better is it silently to gaze wide-eyed, sincere, perplexed into the omnipresent *I-do-not-know*, than to squirrel gyrate in the old vicious circle, or to cob-web life-deep chaos with verbiage, subterfuge, and explanations that do not explain.

Blenheim, cumulatively at least, stands for the first and fatal blow that fortune dealt to her fair haired favorite Louis le Grand. The treaties of Utrecht (1713) and Rastadt (1714) were an appalling humiliation to the Grand Monarch who had imperiously dictated the conditions of Aix-la-Chapelle and Nimeguen.

"There are no longer any Pyrenees", said Louis XIV., arbiter of Europe, as his grandson, a boy of seventeen, was raised to the throne as Philip V. of Spain. And then all Europe flew to arms and for thirteen years blood flowed and war dogs killed one another because that boy was on the throne and Louis' witty words had razed the Pyrenees.

This war is known as the War of the Spanish Succession. A second Grand Alliance was formed; England, Holland, Sweden, Savoy, Austria fought against France. The famous English general, Marlborough, and Prince Eugene of Savoy, in the service of the Emperor, won the memorable battles, Blenheim, Ramillies, Oudenarde and Malplaquet.

The allies chose for the Spanish throne, the Archduke Charles, of Austria, the second son of the Emperor Leopold I.; but when after ten years' fighting there was a vacancy in the imperial line and Archduke Charles suddenly became Emperor of Austria, the allies, fearing the preponderance of Austria in European affairs, withdrew their claim. Philip V. grandson of Louis XIV., was permitted to remain upon the throne of Spain.

The war ended disadvantageously for France. Philip V. was obliged to renounce his claims to the succession in France, so that France and Spain might never be under the same monarch; and thus by miracle-words the august Pyrenees were reinstated (of course they had been deeply disturbed and were, in consequence, duly grateful!); England obtained Gibraltar and the island Minorca; the Duke of Savoy was rewarded with the island Sicily, and Austria obtained Milan, Naples, Sardinia, and part of the Netherlands.

Thirteen years of bloodshed for the whim of an ambitious old man! And thousands fell on both sides, who if questioned, could not honestly have told why they were killing one another.

> "'Now tell us all about the war,
> And what they fought each other for?'
> Young Peterkin he cries,
> While little Wilhelmine looks up
> with wonder waiting eyes."
>
> * * * * *
>
> "'It was the English', Caspar said,
> Who put the French to rout,
> But what they fought each other for—
> I couldn't well make out:
> But things like that, you know, must be
> At every famous victory."
>
> —*Southey.*

And the world is as fatuous as Southey's old "Caspar", and we of the awakening twentieth century are sorely perplexed "Peterkins". Why must things like that be; and why do men speak of successful human slaughter as a "famous victory"; and why do martial music and blare of trumpet and drum and epaulettes and ribbons and medals and barbaric pomp in general—succeed in silencing the death groans and in hiding from view the bloody agonies and the demon horrors of the battlefield?

> "Why 'twas a very wicked thing"
> Quoth little Wilhelmine.
> "Nay, nay, my little girl", said he,
> "It was a famous victory."
> "But what good came of it at last"?
>
> * * * * *
>
> "Why, that I cannot tell", said he,
> "But 'twas a famous victory."

And the voice of the questioning child is lost in answerless fatuity. When will the world hear and honestly answer?

LOUIS XIV.

Louis le Grand, greatest of the Bourbons, lived too long. For seventy-two years

(1643-1775) Louis was king and for, at least, fifty years his power was absolute.

Louis' long reign had as contemporary English history the disastrous Civil War and the beheading of Charles I. (1649); the Cromwellian Protectorate (1653); the Restoration of the Stuarts (1660); the reign of the Merry Monarch, the misfortunes of James II., the revolution of 1688, the battle of the Boyne, and the final deposition and expulsion of James II.; the accession to the throne of England as King William III., of Louis' most inveterate foe, William, Prince of Orange (1688); the death of King William III. (1702); the reign of Queen Anne, her death, and the beginning of the House of Hanover (1715).

On the continent the Thirty Years' War was happily ended by the treaty of Westphalia (1648). Peter the Great ascended the throne of Russia (1682). In the great battle of Pultowa (1709) the power of Sweden was practically annihilated; the madly victorious career of Charles XII. of Sweden was stopped, and his successes together with the more solid attainments of his predecessor, Gustavus Adolphus, were rendered negative; Russia advanced over her prostrate foe to her place among the nations.

For forty years success, pleasure, honor, power, and glory beamed in full radiance upon Louis—both as man and monarch. Had he died even as late as 1702 when William, his great rival foe, died, Louis would have been, to all appearances, the most blessed of mortals and his reign the most glorious in the annals of France.

If Pompey the Great had died on his triumphal return from the Mithradatic war, his life would have been esteemed singularly happy and free from the reverses and misfortunes that are the ordinary lot of mortals. But Pompey lived to see all his blushing honors grow gray, as the admiring eyes that had once adoringly gazed upon Pompey the Great turned from him, the setting sun, to the dazzling effulgence of the rising orb, Caius Julius Cæsar. Pharsalia lay in that alienating gaze and assassination and bloody death.

The last years of Louis XIV. were burdened with many miseries. His fortitude and magnanimity under these crushing blows form, perhaps, his best claim to the title *Great*. The War of the Spanish Succession ended with the humiliating treaty of Utrecht. Blenheim, Ramillies, Oudenarde, Malplaquet had, in great measure, swept away all that the successful years had, with blood and treasure, attained. But it was in his domestic relations that the aged monarch was most sorely afflicted. The Dauphin died, and a few months later his second son, the Duke of Burgundy, Fenelon's favorite pupil, died; Adelaide of Savoy, wife of the Duke of Burgundy, soon followed her husband to the grave; their two sons yet lived, and of these, the elder, a promising youth, died suddenly and there remained only a delicate infant—the future Louis XV.

Louis bore all these sorrows with fortitude and sublime resignation. In the same stoic or heroic attitude of mind he looked forward into the gathering darkness of death. There is something truly great in the man who can suffer cataclysmic misfortunes and deny to himself the relief of a cry of complaint.

Louis died calmly at Versailles, Sept. 1, 1715. His last words were to his little grandson, a frail boy of five years; sadly the dying monarch said, "My child, you are about to become a great king. Do not imitate me either in my taste for building or in my love of war. Endeavor on the contrary to live in peace with the neighboring nations. Render to God all that you owe to him and cause his name to be honored by your subjects. Strive also to relieve the burdens of your people which I myself have been unable to do."

And with this futile advice carrying with it his own confession of failure Louis le Grand died. The king is dead—long live the king!

CHAPTER XIV.
PULTOWA

Russia came into existence as a nation on the day of the victory of the Muscovite troops under Peter the First over the Swedes and allies under Charles XII. of Sweden, at Pultowa, A.D. 1709. What Russia has attained to since that date is known and startling significant; what she was previous to that date is insignificant.

As Creasy says: "Yet a century and a half (two centuries) have hardly elapsed since Russia was first recognized as a member of the drama of modern European history—, previous to the battle of Pultowa, Russia played no part. Charles V. and his great rival (Francis I.), our Elizabeth and her adversary Philip of Spain, the Guises, Sully, Richelieu, Cromwell, De Witt, William of Orange, and the other leading spirits of the sixteenth and seventeenth centuries, thought no more about the Muscovite Czar than we now think about the King of Timbuctoo."

Sweden lost on that dread day when "fortune fled the royal Swede", all that she had toilsomely gained thro' the slow centuries. At one blow her fairest provinces were torn from her; and the rival Russian throne ascended to European prominence over the prostrate power of Sweden.

Peter the Great even upon the field of victory fully realized that Pultowa was for him the key to the Baltic. Even amid the carnage of the slaughter-field where ten thousand men lay dying or dead and the Vorksla river ran red, his eagle gaze beheld the Russia resultant from the Treaty of Nystadt. Exultantly he cried out that "the sun of the morning had fallen from Heaven, and the foundation of St. Petersburg at length stood firm."

From dread Pultowa's day even to the hour, Russia has steadily advanced by slow, gigantic strides unto a dominating prominence among the family of nations. The cabinets of Turkey, Austria, Germany, Italy, France, and England are secretly tho' effectively influenced by Russia.

REPUBLIC OR EMPIRE.

Napoleon said that all Europe would ultimately become either Muscovite or Republican. Which shall it be? The answer as deduced from present tendencies might be—Republican: but no thoughtful observer can fail to regard attentively and apprehensively that sullen Sclavonic dominance extending insidiously and simultaneously into India, Persia, Mongolia, Turkey, the Balkans, and Central Europe.

Amalgamation, the mergence of the many into one, sameness—quiescent and content under a powerful, capable, and just administration, seem to be and ever to have been the ideal form of government. The empires of the past—Egyptian, Babylonian, Persian, Grecian, Roman; the Holy Roman Empire and the Socialistic commune of the future—all include as fundamental principle this solidarity. So far, indeed, it has proved a marsh-light leading to the marsh; but we dream that it will yet lead out of and beyond the muddy, bloody marsh and ultimately light up millennial realms of world-wide oneness, goodness, gladness, peace.

CHARLES XII. OF SWEDEN.

When Charles set out on that expedition having for its object the castigation and possible subjugation of the upstart Tartar hordes weakly held together by Peter of Russia,—all Europe believed that Charles would briefly and successfully accomplish that object.

Sweden was then a power for whose alliance and friendly interest the most powerful monarchs of Europe contended. Louis XIV. of France sought the aid of Charles in the war then waging between France and England; and Marlborough, leader of the English forces in France, went personally to the court of Charles in order to solicit that monarch's aid or at least his neutrality in the great struggle then in progress.

Charles himself was fully confident of victory; and in his romantic plans drawn up for the future, the overthrow of Peter formed only an episode. A year, perhaps, would be required for the full accomplishment of the Russian enterprise; then he, Charles of Sweden, victor of Moscow and arbiter from the Kremlin, would hastily return to western Europe and begin preparations on a gigantic scale for his master-achievement—the dethronement of the Pope of Rome, and the demolition of the Papacy.

Desire-dream of many; achievement of none: for this magic Gibraltar elusively endures bearing its age-old scars as brightest ornamentations. Charles XII. did not, indeed, attack Rome; but did Pultowa save the Papacy? No: the missiles of the Madman of the North whether hurled in the real or only in that futile future plan, would have been equally ineffectual; the magic rock would, perhaps bear another scar bright shining today as trophy of its past struggle and victory.

The lesson of history would seem to teach mortals to expect the unexpected. At Saratoga, at Valmy, at Pultowa, in the Teutoberger Wald, at Marathon, and at Babylon—the undreamed of, the altogether unanticipated, unprepared for, both by the combatants themselves and the world-spectators—took place.

Charles XII., who had set out from Sweden with an army of eighty-five thousand men, Swedes and allies, escaped from the shambles of Pultowa only by swimming across a river red with blood and thus reaching an alien shore weak, wounded, a fugitive, and comparatively alone. Eighty-five thousand men died for the gratification of the personal ambition of the Swedish king; and, by the irony of fate, for the ruination of their native land and the aggrandizement of Peter the First, subsequently and, perhaps, consequently Peter the Great, of Russia.

SCLAVONIC VERSUS TEUTONIC.

The battle of Pultowa was the first decisive victory of the Sclavonic race over the Germanic. Arnold, in his *Lectures on Modern History*, says that the last chapter of the history of Europe will narrate the achievements leading to Muscovite ascendency and the glories of world-dominant Panslavism.

Do nations and races attain only to a certain degree of excellence and then deteriorate? And is that the plan fatefully fixed for the planet Earth? Mycenæ, Troy, Philæ, Babylon, Athens make answer in the affirmative.

A poem, *Christ in the Universe*, by Alice Meynell comes to mind. In a few master touches the writer describes God's way of revealing Himself to us mortals:

"With the ambiguous earth
His dealings have been told us; these abide:
The signal to a maid, the human birth,
The lesson, and the Young Man crucified."

But do the other planets of our solar system, do the stars, those countless suns controlling countless planets—know aught of God's way of dealing with our Earth? Or can we even in loftiest flight of thought conceive "in what guise He walked the Pleiades, the Lyre, the Bear?"

Then the good glad confidence of the soul in touch with God, in tune with the Infinite, in Te Deum ecstasy of exultation, overflows in the concluding lines:

"Oh, be prepared, my soul;
To read the unconceivable, to scan
The million forms of God those stars unroll
When in our turn we show to them—a Man."

They are indeed blessed in whom dwells this abiding confidence, and for whom at times at least, there is overflow in Te Deum exaltation. The slaughter-fields of history and rivers rolling red; the answerless Whys wailing from out the past forlorn as Pharaoh-ghosts in search of non-existent mummies; the chaos of it all, from Memphis to modern Cairo; the damnable wrongs, the demon cruelties, the awful sufferings, the hellish horrors—all sound sonoral in orchestral harmony when faith and hope and good glad confidence play dominant and the soul is exultant in God.

DEATH OF CHARLES.

Charles XII. never rallied from the defeat of Pultowa. He did, indeed, linger for a time in Turkey, striving to enlist the sympathies of the Sultan in his behalf. And history relates that at last the Sultan yielded to the importunities of Charles, and that an army was fitted out for the invasion of Russia: but the command of the forces was entrusted to the Vizier, not to Charles. And the story runs that the Russians were completely trapped by the Turkish troops and Pultowa seemed about to be avenged and the hand of destiny turned backward; when Catherine, later the wife of Peter the Great and first Empress of Russia, seeing the hopelessness of exit from the trap into which the Russians had fallen, went secretly by night into the tent of the Grand Vizier, and by her charms, and by her gifts of gold, diamonds, and pearls bribed the stern old soldier so that he failed to see the following day that the Russians were secretly stealing away from the trap in which he had caught them.

Charles withdrew to Sweden and, a war having broken out between Norway and Sweden, he was killed at the siege of Frederickshall: but just how he met death is not authoritatively known. He was found dead in the trenches the night preceding the battle.

Voltaire has sympathetically told the story of Charles XII. of Sweden. His meteoric career has often been used, as Johnson happily said, "to point a moral or adorn a tale." He ranks with Alexander and Napoleon in personal magnetism, in phenomenal attainment, and in the ultimate loss and evanishment of all attained. His name and fame are ever subtly suggestive of—

> Dread Pultowa's day
> When fortune left the royal Swede;
> Around a slaughtered army lay
> No more to combat and to bleed;
> The power and fortune of the war
> Had passed to the triumphant Czar.
>
> —*Byron.*

CHAPTER XV.
SARATOGA

The surrender of General Burgoyne at Saratoga, though not, perhaps, properly classed among battles, is, nevertheless, properly classed among events momentous in their influence upon the destinies of nations. Looking upon the American Revolution as a whole and from a dispassionate distance, Burgoyne's surrender at Saratoga is seen to be the fateful turning of the tide which rolled from crest-wave English victory back to slow but sure English discomfiture and ultimate defeat.

As a result of the Colonial victory at Saratoga came recognition of *the Independent United States of America*, first from France, later from Spain, and still later from Holland. Confidence was established; untried troops had stood breast to breast against veterans of the British army, against skilled Grenadiers, and these untried troops had won; they had caused the proud British general to retreat from place to place, they had surrounded him at last on Saratoga Heights and forced him to capitulate. The independence of the thirteen original states and all evolutionary Republican America lay potential in the victory of Generals Gates and Arnold over Burgoyne and his veterans at Saratoga.

PLAN.

"The best laid plans of mice and men
Gang aft agley."

—Burns.

Burgoyne's plan was good; and had not General St. Leger failed to capture Fort Stanwix and then to proceed along the Mohawk to its confluence with the Hudson and there join his force to that of Burgoyne; and had not General Baum failed to win the battle of Bennington and so secure the magazines of provisions so sorely needed by the British army; and had not Lord Howe considered it more advantageous to cross over to the Delaware and attack Philadelphia, rather than remain at New York ready for emergency; and had not General Clinton been retarded in his victorious advance up from Albany; if all, or perhaps any one of these conditions had been the reverse of what they were, why, history might be the reverse of what it is.

Momentous little things—so seeming trifling, inconsequential, negligible—and yet potential of cataclysmic calamity! An insect bores into the heart of an oak, and the forest monarch falls: a tiny trickling rill freezes in the rock and the mountain is rent asunder; a pine twig breaks under its weight of snow and the awful avalanche comes crashing down. In the moral world, too, the results seem altogether out of proportion to the cause: a glance of suspicion and the bloom of perfect trust is gone from the heart forever; an unkind word and love withers, a deed—it dies; one lie, one little wormy lie, and the fair integrity of character has in it the boring insect with which it may, indeed, flourish full foliage for a season, but by which, in the end, it must, being hollow hearted, succumb to the storm and fall and die.

Perhaps when Burgoyne sent for the Indians and made them part of his fighting force, he then admitted into his moral makeup, as well as his military, the mighty *little thing* which should silently yet forcefully work disaster. For many men who were irresolute as to which side to join, being indeed loyal at heart to the mother country and hesitating to strike against her, boldly threw in their fortunes with the Colonists when they heard that the Red Man formed part of the force of the advancing army. They knew what savage warfare meant even better than Burgoyne knew. Many are inclined to excuse Burgoyne on the plea that he knew nothing of the horrible atrocities of the Indians when intoxicated with the blood of battle: but fate did not excuse him. His Indians never knew the intoxication of victorious battle—thanks to the stern resolution of men who fought in defence of mothers, sisters, wives, and children shuddering in nearby homes: and as defeat came and ignominious retreat from post to post before the enraged advance of a conquering foe, the Indians deserted the army and slunk away through the western wilds back to their native tribes.

BENEDICT ARNOLD.

Strange that history remembers only Arnold the Traitor and not Arnold the hero of Ticonderoga, Quebec, and Saratoga. Too bad he didn't die in that brilliant charge upon Burgoyne's intrenchments, where after overcoming all obstacles and apparently just on the point of victory he was wounded in the same leg that had been painfully injured in the assault on Quebec—and carried fainting and profusely bleeding from the field. To be twice wounded for a cause and then to betray it—perverse human heart, who shall know its depths of perversity!

And yet the events since that time, which Arnold could not foresee or foreknow, rather than the concomitant circumstances of that time, which Arnold saw and knew, have proclaimed him Traitor. And had the results been otherwise, had not his own mad efforts helped turn the tide at Saratoga, Arnold might now be known as a shrewdly diplomatic young officer who, influenced by a beautiful Tory wife and seeing the cause of the Colonists desperate, had timely transferred his allegiance to the British army and bravely helped along the conquering cause of the mother country.

And Major Andre sleeps in honored rest in old Westminster Abbey; while the man twice wounded in battle, the hero of Ticonderoga, Quebec, and Saratoga sleeps in an unhonored grave having as epitaph indelibly traced upon surrounding air and earth and water and sky—Arnold the Traitor.

GENERAL FRAZER.

SARATOGA

General Frazer was mortally wounded in the engagement which took place October 7th. He died in camp the following day. The Italian historian Botta gives the following account of his burial. "Toward midnight, the body of General Frazer was buried in the British camp. His brother officers assembled sadly around while the funeral service was read over the remains of their brave comrade, and his body was committed to the hostile earth. The ceremony, always mournful and solemn of itself, was rendered even terrible by the sense of recent losses, of present and future dangers, and of regret for the deceased. Meanwhile, the blaze and roar of the American artillery amid the natural darkness and stillness of the night came on the senses with startling awe. The grave had been dug within range of the enemy's batteries; and while the service was proceeding, a cannon ball struck the ground close to the coffin, and spattered earth over the face of the officiating chaplain."

There is something painfully pathetic in the scene thus presented to the imagination. War has no respect for the rights of the living or the dying or the dead.

SURRENDER.

On the 13th of October, 1777, General Burgoyne, besieged by overpowering numbers on the heights of Saratoga and seeing that his army was facing disease and famine, and being unable to establish communication either with Lord Howe or with General Clinton—opened negotiations with General Gates as to conditions of surrender.

At first General Gates demanded that the royal army should surrender themselves prisoners of war. Burgoyne refused.

It was later agreed upon that "the troops under General Burgoyne were to march out of their camp with the honors of war, and the artillery—of the entrenchments, to the verge of the river, where the arms and the artillery were to be left. The arms to be piled by word of command from their own officers. A free passage was to be granted to the army under Lieutenant General Burgoyne to Great Britain upon condition of not serving again in North America during the present contest."

These conditions having been formally accepted, an army of weak and wounded men laboriously descended the heights and marched out to the place appointed for the laying down of arms. General Gates was on this occasion extremely courteous, and the Colonial troops were soon fraternizing with the English soldiers and striving in every way to supply their many needs and wants.

General Clinton, who was but fifty miles down the river with supplies and men, heard with dismay of Burgoyne's surrender. Lord Howe's plans were all broken up by this sudden change of fortune. And the far away, sleepily stubborn British Parliament felt the first cold intimation that it might possibly be *wrong* and Burke might possibly be *right* in their respective estimates of the rebel children in the wide awake, wonderful New World.

And so the failure of the New York plans, culminating in Burgoyne's surrender at Saratoga, proved to be one of the mighty *little things* potential of results that change the destinies of nations.

CHAPTER XVI.
VALMY

"Bury my heart in Valmy," said Kellerman, soldier of the Seven Years' War, victor of Valmy, Marshal of France under the first Napoleon, and court favorite of the Bourbons—as the shadows of old-age death deepened into darkness. And they buried his heart in Valmy.

A simple monument on the crest of the hill, the bloodiest spot of the one-time battle ground, tells to the thoughtful stranger the story of a restless heart o'er whom as o'er Madame de Stael and many another heir of a checkered heritage might be engraved as epitaph, "Here rests one who never rested."

The era ushered in by the battle of Valmy was especially prolific of men whose political principles changed violently from one extreme to the other; only to rebound again and again, until, at length, weariness and cynic scorn of good in anything caused them to drift in perplexed acquiescence wherever the tide rolled longest and strongest. Talleyrand, Dumouriez, Marquis de la Rouarie, Kellerman, La Fayette, Mirabeau, Duc de Chartres, and even Napoleon Bonaparte were, in great measure, moulded into their respective historic moulds by the lurid lightning play of antithetic forces ever fatefully flashing and slashing and crashing around them.

SEPTEMBER TWENTIETH.

Yet in August, 1792, when sixty thousand Prussians, and forty thousand Austrians and fifteen thousand of the old French *noblesse* started out upon that "military promenade to Paris": or on the morning of September 20th, when that victoriously advancing column prepared gaily for its first skirmish with the raw revolutionary levies who filled the passes of the Argonne wooded heights and threatened to impede that "promenade"—who could see, or who could dare to dream what the issue of that encounter would be; what results would follow; what rivers of blood would flow; what lordly heads would roll from under the guillotine; what national madness would break out barking at the peace of Europe; what mighty Madman would arise urging on that national madness even to Wagram, Austerlitz, Moscow, Leipsic, Waterloo!

RETRIBUTION.

Had Kellerman failed to come up just in time to join forces with Dumouriez: had the Prussian advance been just an hour or two earlier: had the heavy mists lifted from the Valmy hill and Argonne wood revealing the relative positions of Kellerman and Dumouriez: had the forcing of the defile by Clairfayt and his Austrian corps proved fatally successful: had the Duke of Brunswick resolutely charged a second time up that hill of bristling bayonets: had the King of Prussia, urged on by a vision of the future, authoritatively commanded that the hill be taken and himself led the charge: ah! so we learnedly say from the calm eminence far away, but history is made in the low blind fury of the fray. Perhaps, too, there were potently at work upon that fated battlefield, forces that elude the gaze of the dreamer on the height far away:—a determining animus, moral and spiritual potencies formed by the slow centuries and long controlled, but now liberated and wildly free. Ghosts of ten thousand wrongs may have arisen between the gilded ranks of the French *noblesse* and the ragged rows of the Carmagnoles: and, as the spirits that arose over the tent of Richard the Third, the night before the battle of Bosworth Field, cursed Richard and blessed Richmond; threatened Richard with defeat and death on the morrow and cheered Richmond with hopes and promises of victory; fought intangibly, invisibly, yet potently present amid the awful carnage of Bosworth field even until death trampled down Richard: so, in like manner, may the ghosts of ten thousand wrongs have arisen between the men of the old *regime* and of the rebellious new—fighting for their fellow-wrongs still writhing in the flesh, fighting the old, old fight of retaliation, compensation, stern adjudication, infinite justice. As the sun's rays that reach earth are but one-millionth of the rays emitted by the sun, so for every thing known, bright shining on the historic page, there are a million things unknown.

BATTLE.

About seven o'clock on that battle morn as the mists were dissipating, the successfully united French forces saw with dismay the slowly advancing army of the allies; long lines of Prussian cavalry, Austrian light troops, solid columns of infantry, batteries of artillery filled the valley and moved slowly, sinuously toward the Valmy height.

Dumouriez anxiously scanned the white strained faces of his untried troops. Would they fail him in the crucial hour? Would they break away in panic rout when the death-play began? It was their custom.

"He who fights and runs away
May live to fight another day."

At Tournay, at Lille, and in general throughout the opening campaign this uncertain "heap of shriekers" had fled away as satyrs pursued by Pan when the death-play began. Would the Carmagnoles of today, and, at deepest heart, the *Jacquerie* of many a yesterday, dare to fight face to face and hand to hand against the august *seigneurs* of the old regime—late their dread lords and masters? Three hundred years of culture lay between them.

Of all who took part in the battle that day, either among the allies or the revolutionary forces, perhaps not one realized the full importance of what had taken place as did Johan Wolfgang von Goethe—then a young man and comparatively unknown; he had followed the allies as a spectator, a curious seeker of strange scenes, a bold hot-blood eager as his own Wilhelm Meister to taste adventure at its source and to know the ways of the world in love and in war. Goethe, with the unerring insight of genius, perceived that victory to the Carmagnoles marked a new era. In his own words to comrades in camp on the night following the battle; "From this place and from this day forth commences a new era in the world's history, and you can all say you were present at its birth."

FRANCE A REPUBLIC.

Simultaneously with victory at Valmy, France broke from the cocoon of monarchical forms and proclaimed herself a Republic. Even while the battle was raging, the National Convention in Paris were engaged in this deliberation, this liberation. The Republic of France dates from September 20th, 1792. And under the regrettable excesses of the Revolution, the reactionary repression of the First Empire, of the Bourbon restoration, the revolt of 1830, of 1848, even to Sedan and the hour—the spirit of democracy, of liberty and independence born Sept. 20th, 1792, has flourished and flourishes indestructibly, imperishably.

And yet as Dumouriez said, "France (revolutionary) was within a hair's breadth of destruction." And had victory gone that day to the allies, the throne of Louis XVI. would have been reinstated on foundations so firm that centuries would not shake it. For in La Vendee and throughout Brittany there was at that time a strong uprising in favor of the throne: men such as the admirable old Marquis de la Rouarie were abandoning the Revolutionary cause and turning decisively back to monarchical principles; moreover the recent atrocious September massacres had alienated the more conservative and thoughtful men throughout France. Never was the time more propitious for the return of the mild and humane Louis XVI., the re-establishment of the monarchy, the substitution of Reform for Revolution, and of concessive peace for fratricidal war. But by that hair's breadth republican France won; and that winning mustered out the gentlemanly old regime and ushered in the arrogant awful new.

The spirit of Valmy flies eagle-free over the world today. It is the spirit making possible the face to face and hand to hand fight between the laborer and the capitalist, the soldier and the king, woman and man: and that Spirit tells strange and terrible tales of victory.

CHAPTER XVII.
WATERLOO

Waterloo stands for the sudden darkening of the blazing comet, Napoleon; and for the return of France to the realm of the real after twenty-five years of hysterical unreality. Consequentially, too, Waterloo meant the relaxation of the terrible war-tension which had held rigid both Europe and the civilized world. The victor-trampling of Napoleon's troops was heard on this side of the Atlantic; and our second war with England (1812-1814) was, in great measure, both in origin and in purposeless conclusion, the result of that victor-trampling.

After Waterloo (June 18, 1815) the war-weary world snapped tension and sank to rest; tho' perhaps the secret terror tremor was not utterly stilled until six years later (May 5, 1821) when Napoleon, Man of Destiny, lay dead at St. Helena.

Youth may idolize Napoleon, age may condemn: but so long as human nature is what it is, we ordinary mortals—knowing the difficulties that attend success, eminence, excellence; knowing the almost insuperable obstacles that bar the way to supremacy, be it cosmopolitan, national, provincial, municipal, or parochial—will ever regard with loving wonder the man who won excellence and world-wide supremacy.

It has been said that a base man or a thoroughly selfish man cannot truly love or inspire love. Whom did Napoleon love? History answers *Napoleon*. Yet Napoleon certainly inspired love. Josephine, the army, the Old Guard devotedly loved Napoleon. In the song from the French "To Napoleon" beginning with the line, "Must thou go, my glorious Chief", some ardent admirer lamenting Napoleon's downfall and doom cries out:

> "My chief, my king, my friend, adieu!
> Never did I droop before;
> Never to my sovereign sue,
> As his foes I now implore:
> All I ask is to divide
> Every peril he must brave;
> Sharing by my hero's side
> His fall, his exile, and his grave."

And elsewhere we read that at Napoleon's farewell "all wept, but particularly Savary, and a Polish officer, who had been exalted from the ranks by Bonaparte. He clung to his master's knees; wrote a letter to Lord Keith, entreating permission to accompany him, even in the most menial capacity, which could not be admitted."

Too bad Nap didn't die with the Old Guard. At *La Belle Alliance* in the midst of that last square of his death-devoted friends and lovers Napoleon should have died. "The Guard dies, it does not surrender" replied that gallant band as they awaited the last terrible onslaughts of the victor-breathing troops and thus were they hewn down even to a man. And while this slaughter of his Guard was going on, Napoleon, urged and aided by Marshal Soult, was galloping away from the field. Too bad Napoleon didn't die at Waterloo.

QUATRE-BRAS AND LIGNY.

Hoping to strike a decisive blow at the Prussian forces under Blücher before they could effect a junction with Wellington's advancing army, Napoleon marched upon Ligny (June 16, 1815). He left Marshal Ney at *Quatre-Bras* with instructions to oppose the advance of the English army towards Ligny, and to fight if necessary. Ney, taking advantage of Wellington's temporary absence, (he had ridden across to confer with Blücher and was then hastening back) resolved to attack the Anglo-Netherland forces under the Prince of Orange. He was repulsed; nevertheless he succeeded in checking the advance of the army towards Ligny.

In the meantime Napoleon had gained a victory over eighty thousand Prussian troops under Blücher, and they were even then in ignominious retreat towards Wavre. Napoleon ordered Marshall Grouchy to follow up the Prussians and to prevent them, at any cost, from joining forces with Wellington. Blücher had been wounded at Ligny and his army thoroughly demoralized: Grouchy, with an army of thirty thousand men, seemed more than a match for such an opponent; and doubtless, Napoleon, when hastening away from Ligny to oppose his more formidable foe, felt sure that the Prussians and Blücher were happily eliminated from the conflict confronting him.

But in that conference between Wellington and Blücher, it had been agreed upon that in case of defeat at Ligny, Blücher should retreat towards Wavre, and Wellington would withdraw towards Waterloo; so that they would still be in line of direct communication, and a union of forces might be effected. Wellington and Blücher trusted each other implicitly. "Whether after victory or defeat, come to me at Waterloo," said Wellington. "I will come," answered Blücher grimly and—he came.

The following day (June 17) a reinforcement under Bülow reached Blücher at Wavre; thus the loss sustained at Ligny was made good. At Grouchy's approach the following morning (June 18) Blücher resolved to sacrifice deliberately a regiment of seventeen thousand men in order to detain Grouchy and keep him from returning to Napoleon, while he (Blücher) and Bülow with the bulk of the Prussian army should hasten to the aid of Wellington at Waterloo.

Not at Wavre but at Waterloo was destiny at work; this Blücher knew and he acted accordingly: this Grouchy did not know; and after completely routing with great slaughter the Prussians under Thielman, he kept up a meaningless pursuit following a will-o-the-wisp, whilst Napoleon, after sending to him messenger after messenger urging his aid, stood still at last and deadly pale under the gorgeous June sunset, and saw all his hopes and dreams go down in darkness as the ominous moving cloud emerging from the direction of Wavre and advancing, glitteringly advancing, proved to be Blücher—not Grouchy.

That deliberate leaving of seventeen thousand men as a bait in a trap for the victorious French forces thundering onward from Ligny is typical of the demon ingenuity of war. I have read somewhere that in darkest Africa the lure to the tiger trap is a kid securely fastened. Its fearful bleatings attract the night prowling brute: there is a spring: then awful shrieks arise growing shriller and shriller as the pangs of being devoured alive grow tenser and more terrible: by this time the cannibals are upon the scene and the trap is sprung.

Seventeen thousand soldiers as kid to the tiger lure—and men call themselves civilized! Could a woman do that? No; woman is higher in the moral scale than man. And the higher, thank God, is the kinder, tenderer, the more compassionate. Wars and all hellish machinations of cruelty must cease as the race, as a whole, advances into that higher. And advancement, even tho' zigzag, shall ultimately attain to the higher and even to the highest. We dream so.

KING MAKING VICTORY.

Perhaps no other battlefield of the historic past has been more frequently described or rendered more vivid to mental vision than the field of Waterloo. Victor Hugo's masterly portrayal in *Les Miserables* is doubtless the best; but Sir Walter Scott, Lord Byron, Captain Siborne, and Napoleonic writers *ad infinitum* have added richness of tonal qualities to the monochrome.

Those two long lines of undulating hills running nearly parallel, with a valley half a mile in width between; the allied army under Wellington on the northern ridge, the devoted French forces on the southern; the artillery of each army firing incessantly upon the other over the heads of the combatants in the valley and on the lower slope; the forest of Soignies darkly waving in the rear of Wellington's forces; the village and ravine at the right warding off a possible flank movement; the two hamlets La Haye and Papillote at the left, strongly garrisoned of course and then, too, expectant of Blücher's approach from Wavre; Hougoumont, an old stone chateau surrounded by a copse of beech trees, half way down the slope nearly in front of the British right center—strongly fortified, most important, strategic; Hougoumont—to be taken and retaken seven times during that day of destiny and held at last in flaming ruins by the British; the farm house La Haie Sainte somewhat down from the British left center, heavily garrisoned, expectant of what came; the French forces in superb battle array on the Charleroi crest of the hill, with an open way to France behind them and the hamlet La Belle Alliance, Napoleon's headquarters, and their idol Napoleon—before: why every school-boy knows the plan of this most famous battlefield!

Had Napoleon's star not been fatally descendant he must have won at Waterloo. His forces, seventy-two thousand, were numerically stronger than the opposing forces seventy-one thousand eight hundred and five, under Wellington; then, too, his army was a unit and unanimously devoted to him, whereas Wellington's army was a mixup of Belgians, Dutch, Nassauers, Brunswickers, Hanoverians, with only twenty-four thousand English troops upon whom he could implicitly rely. Wellington knew and Napoleon knew that the Belgian and Netherland forces would far rather be fighting under the French eagles than against them. And in truth these regiments did disgracefully run away from before the advancing French columns in the crisis of the strife, and the demoralizing effect of their flight was counteracted only by the superhuman efforts and life-sacrificing devotedness of England's two brave heroes Picton and Ponsonby.

It is true that Wellington confidently awaited a strong Prussian reinforcement, eighty thousand—and Blücher. It is equally true that owing to heavy rainfall and consequently almost impassable roads between Wavre and Waterloo, Blücher who was eagerly looked for at 3 p. m. did not reach the field until 7 p. m. and at that time the battle was practically won by the British.

Had Napoleon's pristine favor been accorded him—the magic favor of fate that had made possible Areola, Rivoli, Jena, Ulmn, Wagram, Austerlitz—he would have defeated Wellington at Waterloo, advanced upon the advancing Prussians and completely routed them; and then he would have hastened to crush separately and before a junction could be effected the various contingencies of the Coalition even then converging upon him by way of the Rhine, the Alps, and the Pyrenees. But fate forsook her favorite at Waterloo. Olympian Zeus, jealous of Promethean man, has decreed that if once, then certainly not *twice*, shall a mortal transcend the lot of mortals.

It rained all night long that memorable seventeenth of June, the night before the battle. Of those forces that thus drearily bivouacked upon the opposing hills, some fifty thousand men thus passed their last night upon earth. Nature wept for them. The skies dissolved in tears at the mad folly of mortals. Rain, inconsolable rain, fell from the early afternoon of the seventeenth, thro' all the night, and sobbingly drizzled late on the morning of the eighteenth as the armies went out to battle.

That dreary last night of life for fifty thousand men—what did it mean to them! Did any flint-glitterings, struck out of sullen gloom, zigzag thro' the darkness of their minds? Why should they fight? Why should they kill and be killed on the morrow? Wellington, Napoleon—what were they to the common soldier; he would be free, he would go to his home, he would live his life as God gave it to him to live. Desert on the eve of battle! Ah, no! Yet, why not?

"So free we seem, so fettered fast we are." Honor bound tonight and death bound tomorrow night! Who of those sleeping in yonder tents, under the rain, shall fall tomorrow? Whom shall he kill? Who may kill—him?

"Some one has blundered."

* * * * *

"Theirs not to make reply,
Theirs not to reason why,

Theirs but to do and die."

Again, why? Half a million men must die because Napoleon blundered—Why! And the tears of the rain made answer.

At half past eleven o'clock Sunday morning, June 18, shortly after the village church bells had ceased ringing, the French forces began descending the slope of the southern ridge and were soon dashing across the valley. Their first object was the capture of Hougoumont. In the words of Creasy: "Napoleon began the battle by directing a powerful force from his left wing under his brother, Prince Jerome, to attack Hougoumont. Column after column of the French now descended from the west of the southern heights, and assailed that post with fiery valor, which was encountered with the most determined bravery. The French won the copse round the house, but a party of British Guards held the house itself throughout the day. Amid shell and shot, and the blazing fragments of part of the buildings, this obstinate contest was continued. But still the English held Hougoumont, tho' the French occasionally moved forward in such numbers as enabled them to surround and mask this post with part of their troops from their left wing, while others pressed onward up the slope, and assailed the British right."

The fight then became general all along the line. As the French advanced to the left center the Dutch and Belgians under Blyant threw down their arms and fled from the field, whether as result of fright, disinclination to fight, or treachery will, perhaps, never be known. The second line consisted of two brigades of English infantry and with these the gallant Picton charged the advancing French columns already flushed with victory. Volley after volley thinned the advancing ranks and then, at the opportune moment, the British made a fierce bayonet charge. The French reeled back in confusion, halted, and staggering tried to rally, but just then a brigade of English Cavalry rushed down upon them. Two thousand French soldiers were taken prisoners, the artillery-men of Ney's seventy-four advanced guns were sabered and the guns rendered useless. The British cut the throats of the horses of the artillery wagons, and severing the traces, left these poor brutes maddened with pain to add to the horror of the slaughter. In this charge Picton fell.

At La Haie Sainte, the fortified farm house that served as protection of the British left wing, the French performed prodigies of valor. At last Donzelot's infantry gained possession of this long desired point of vantage.

About 4 o'clock a corps of Prussians under Bülow made its appearance at the French right. This disconcerted Napoleon's plan of general assault on the allied center. He sent ten thousand men under Lobau to hold Bülow in check.

In the meantime, Wellington ordered another assault to be made for the re-capture of La Haie Sainte. Ney repelled this attack, but sent for reinforcements. Napoleon sent him the cuirassiers under Milhaud. By mistake the forces of light cavalry under Lefebvre-Desnouettes joined the cuirassiers and hastened to the assistance of La Haie Sainte. Ney finding himself in command of two powerful bodies of horse resolved to take the offensive; he accordingly renewed the attack upon the British center. Wellington had arranged his men in squares; these hedged in with bayonets presented an almost impenetrable front to the enemy. Still they showed signs of wavering; and Ney seeing his advantage sent hurriedly for a reinforcement of infantry; Napoleon could send no more.

Lobau had succeeded in driving Bülow out of the village (Planchenoit) on the French right; La Haie Sainte was still in the possession of the French; and could Ney have obtained the infantry he desired, historians agree that he would have succeeded in forcing the British center. That hour was the pivotal beam of the battle and it seemed about to dip in favor of France.

Nap watched the scene from the opposite hill. How his heart must have thrilled to the air of old time victory; Wagram, Austerlitz,—Waterloo!

It was evening, the western sky was crimson with sunset, night must soon come and end the conflict. Wellington, too, was ardently longing that "the night would come or—Blücher."

And just then on the ominous French right whence Bülow's division had been routed an hour ago, another darkly moving mass of men appeared. Was it Grouchy—hope! or Blücher—despair! It was Blücher. Napoleon turned deadly pale; he asked for a glass of water but in his agitation, he spilled more than half the contents ere his trembling hand could lift the glass to his lips. Thus bitterly began Napoleon's Waterloo.

Napoleon concentrated all his available forces, the reserve troops, and the Old Guard for one more Herculean attack upon the British. Across the plain they dashed, Ney leading the charge, and over their heads played the French artillery in an incessant rain of lead upon the opposing height. Men there were falling under it like leaves in autumn. Wellington, observing the havoc wrought by the French guns, ordered the British Guards to lie prone upon the earth so as to be out of range of the bullets. As the French approached the foot of the ridge, and even as they advanced up the slope, the fire from Napoleon's headquarters continued, but when they had fairly gained the height, the French guns ceased firing.

On rushed the devoted French columns led by Ney, *bravest of the brave*, who, covered with blood and dust, hatless, with clothing torn, and on foot—five horses having been shot under him—still dared to dream of victory. As the French reached the top of the hill, for one madly exultant moment they thought that the enemy had fled; but at Wellington's hissing command, "Up, Guards, and at them!", they stood aghast as the very earth seemed to open and pour out brigade after brigade of British Red Coats. The onslaught was awful. Over the crest of the hill and far down the slope the French were driven saber-slaughtered and slaughtering. *La Garde Reculée* (The Guard is repulsed)—this cry with its ominous suggestion sped from blanched lip to lip. And soon the most desperate of all defeat cries *Sauve qui peut!* (All's lost: save himself who can!) became general among the fleeing French forces.

At La Belle Alliance Napoleon attempted to make a rallying point; he hastily pressed his few devoted followers into a square, declaring it his intention to perish with them. But as it is the surgeon that has most mercilessly used his knife upon others, who shrinks back in awful dread from the knife as used upon himself: so Napoleon who had seen thousands of soldiers die of bloody wounds, could not endure for himself that which he had been willing to witness in others. As the English drew near and, seeing the hopelessness of the French position, called upon them to surrender; and even as General Cambronne gallantly replied, "The Guard dies; it does not surrender", Napoleon spurred back his horse, turned, and galloped at full speed from the field.

EXILE.

Napoleon a second time signed a treaty of abdication just one hundred days after his flagrant violation of the first treaty of abdication. One hundred days of doubtful triumph and then—Waterloo: was it worth while!

The Machiavellian principles—honorable fraud; splendid rascality; a ruler should combine the qualities of the fox and the lion; no matter what the means may be, the vulgar are ever caught by appearances and judge only by the event—which Napoleon had so deeply imbibed from perusal of his favorite book *Il Principe*, suffered sudden collapse of inflation and wraith-like glimmered as will-o-the-wisps in a bog. That stripping away of names and epithets and phrases and opinions and customs and sunlight success from the—Lie: and that Lie in naked hideousness black-branded on the soul for self and all the world to see;—how terrible a triumph of the unseen over the seen, the real over the apparent, the truth over the lie! What Austerlitz concealed Waterloo revealed. Outlaw of Europe, execrable wretch, vile miscreant whom no promises or vows could hold in honor, etc., were among the uncouth Teutonic free translations of Nap's subtly soft *Il Principe*.

And Josephine was dead; she had died a year ago while Nap was at Elba. Josephine never knew the worst about Napoleon; she never could have known the "execrable wretch" as the Congress of Vienna knew him. Love and hate see differently the same objects. As she would gladly have followed Nap to Elba, so, too, would she have been a pitying angel at his side in the world-execration after Waterloo, and in the bitter loneliness of St. Helena. Was Nap, the real, what he was as known and loved by Josephine or what he was as seen and hated by the Congress of Vienna; or neither?

That portrait of Napoleon by Delaroche comes to mind. We are sorry for Nap in his hour of ignominy; we forgive him all the sorrows that he caused—to others; we look with him fascinated into the fatal future, we grieve with the stoic grief of the Man of Destiny.

Meissonier's companion pictures "1807: Friedland" and "1814: Retreat from Moscow" come to mind. Full success-sun convergent from Austerlitz, Jena, Wagram shines in "1807"; penumbral shadows gray-flecked with snows from Borodino, Moscow, Berizina lower in "1814".

Louis David's statuesque picture "Napoleon Crossing the Alps" comes to mind. It seems the "French Revolution on horse-back" yet controlled, goaded up the ascent, led out from bleeding France, and destiny-plunging on towards Italy, Prussia, Austria, Russia.

David's canvas "Coronation of Napoleon and Josephine" comes sadly to mind.

From that rhapsody of color-splendor to bleak Helena surf-lashed by the sea; from that act of crowning exaltation to the signing of abdication at Fontainebleau; from that supreme success in life to a failure-grave under the willows: ah! surely there throbs within and between these antithetic scenes all that enigmatic life may hold for us mortals. Nothing exists beyond—in pleasure or in pain, in honor or dishonor, in success or failure, in highest or lowest.

COR NE EDITO (EAT NOT THE HEART).

Napoleon spent the last six years of life on the island St. Helena (Oct. 16, 1815—May 5, 1821). There are various stories told as to his bitter loneliness whilst in exile, his ceaseless repining at fate, his chafing chagrin under the cautious coldness of Sir Hudson Lowe. Nap is most frequently represented walking alone on the shore, his hands locked behind, his head lowered and his "broad brow oppressive with his mind" bent sullenly forward. Again as a caged eagle he stands for hours at a time on the rocky ledge looking out over the gray waste of waters with eyes straining towards France. And old ocean always inimical to Napoleon and coldly conscious of Aboukir and Trafalgar enjoys indifferently its final triumph. True to Britannia, Ruler of the Wave, the gray waters roll impenetrable to bribery or betrayal, impervious to sentiment or sympathy. Napoleon, victor of a hundred fields, king-maker, arbiter of Europe, is caught and caged; his eagle wings all torn and bleeding yet dash against the bars; he is eating his heart, O restless sea, and he gazes on thee: old ocean rolled responseless.

Am I tonight participant in the woe that had its hours of agony one hundred years ago? It seems so.

HERO WORSHIP.

Balance is hard. And to see clearly all sides of a subject, however conducive to balance, is destructive of enthusiasm. Hero worship is, perhaps, a phase of hysteria, but without it there are no heroes. No name upon the historic page, from Homer's Achilles down to Carlyle's Cromwell, but shines with luster luminous from hero worship. Alexander, Hannibal, Cæsar, Charlemagne, Napoleon—the world will ever love them, not perhaps for what they were, but for the vision splendid with which they are attended, and which was formed and fitted to them by admiring love.

RETROSPECT.

As Nap paced sleeplessly his rock kingdom under the flaky stars, did memory ever conjure up a strange night scene in old Vincennes? The young Duc d'Enghien, last of the race of the great Conde, was asleep in bed. Suddenly, by order of the First Consul, the French soldiery aroused the sleeper, dragged him from his luxurious couch, hurried him across the French frontier, tried him by a military commission, and then, in a ditch of the castle grounds, that very night, by order of the First Consul, they shot to death the gay young man. And they tied a lantern to his breast that it might serve as target to his heart. Did Nap see that night scene from under the flaky stars of St. Helena? His *Memoires* do not so record.

Did the treacherously yielding waves that lapped his island home ever suggest to Nap that horror scene, when after Austerlitz, as the fleeing enemy were escaping over the frozen lake, the French artillery, by order of the Emperor, played heavily upon the ice; it cracked, broke, crashed down, and thousands sank within the treacherous waves. Or did they softly sigh of Berezina, when the heavily laden bridge broke down and his own devoted soldiers and friends—those who had stood by him at Borodino, in Moscow, and in the dread Retreat—struggled in the icy waters? Nap's *Memoires* do not so record.

And the dark rolling billows surf-capped—did they at times suggest low mounds in churchyards, or ominous ridges on recent battle grounds? Half a million men had died that Nap might rise and—fall. All Europe, from Lisbon to Moscow was dotted with their graves. Surely in the retrospective leisure of exile, however it may have been in the fever of the empire-strife, there was regret for all the young life suddenly darkened into death; there was awakening self-knowledge regretful, remorseful; there was lamentation at the futility of it all, the horror, the agony, the shame; there was prayer, the bitter prayer of Thais of the Desert, "Thou who hast made me have mercy on me!" Maybe: not ours to know the enigmatic heart of man; we only say there is no record of such feelings in Nap's memoirs.

Did the year 1809 loom sullen in retrospect? That year held in record the capture of Pope Pius VII. and his confinement at Savona; the ban of excommunication pronounced against Napoleon by his illustrious prisoner; and Nap's divorce from Josephine.

The Emperor was at this time at the height of his career. He was drunk with power. In his hand as playthings were the kingdoms of Europe, and he awarded them as whim or pleasure urged. To his brother Joseph, too scrupulous to be great, Nap condescendingly gave the throne of Spain; to his brother Louis, Holland; to his brother Jerome, Westphalia; to a favorite general, Bernadotte, Sweden; to Murat, Naples. At his touch, the Holy Roman Empire—no longer, indeed, either holy or Roman or an empire—had crumbled into dust. Germany lay prostrate; Austria humbled; Russia chastened, yet friendly. Only England, secure in her watery kingdom, dared to oppose his plans and resist his power.

And then this madman on the dizzy height dreamed a glorious dream. The Pontiff, Pius VII., prisoner at Savona, would annul the marriage with Josephine; then he would marry the sister of the Tsar of Russia; then with the help of Russia he would conquer India and "so strike England to the heart." After that "it will be possible to settle everything and have done with this business of Rome and the Pope. The cathedral of Paris will become that of the Catholic world." And Napoleon shall be all in all. Perhaps, too, this rhapsody ended half audibly with the adulatory words of the prefect of Arras, "God created Napoleon and then rested from His works."

But as seen from gray Helena, the Pope did not annul the marriage with Josephine, nor did Nap marry the sister of Tsar Alexander or long retain the friendship of Russia; nor did he conquer India and so strike England to the heart; nor did he ever have done with that business of Rome and the Pope. That "business" has seen the rise and fall of many—and yet shall see.

Was Napoleon a Catholic? He died in the bosom of the Catholic church after having devoutly received the sacraments. To General Montholon he said: "I was born in the Catholic religion; I wish to fulfil the duties it imposes and to receive the succors it administers." On another occasion he said, "It would rest my soul to hear Mass." These words having been reported to the Pontiff, Pope Pius VII., one time prisoner at Savona, the gentle old man immediately petitioned the English government to send a priest to minister to the spiritual wants of Napoleon. In compliance with the papal request the Abbe Vignali was sent to St. Helena.

Napoleon in his *Memoires*, speaking of Pius VII., calls him "an old man full of tolerance and light"; and in euphemistic reference to his troubles with the pontiff he writes, "Fatal circumstances embroiled our cabinets; I regret it exceedingly."

But whatever Nap may have been in exile at St. Helena, certainly in 1809-10, as arbiter of Europe, he was an arch enemy to the Catholic church, and he acted in flagrant violation of all that the Church stands for. And had his phenomenal success continued to favor him, he would, without doubt, have lived and died an enemy to the Church.

Napoleon never ceased to be a deist. "Who made all that, Gentlemen?" he said one night as he and his friends were gazing at the starry heavens. As a statesman he perceived that religion is an ally to good government, and doubtless he was sincere when he said, "A society without religion is like a ship without a compass; there is no good morality without religion." Nap's re-establishment of the Church in France after the Revolution, and the Concordat made in the beginning of his reign; the six years spent at St. Helena and his death there, would seem to testify that Napoleon was at deepest heart a sincere child of that Church so tolerant of human frailty and so divinely compassionate towards those who come contritely back from error's devious ways and would sleep the last sleep in her bosom.

LET WARS CEASE.

"The drying up a single tear has more
Of honest fame than shedding seas of gore.
And why? because it brings self-approbation:
Whereas the other, after all its glare,
Shouts, bridges, arches, pensions from a nation,
Which (it may be) has not much left to spare,
A higher title or a loftier station,
Tho' they may make Corruption gape or stare,
Yet in the end, except in Freedom's battles—
Are nothing but a child of Murder's rattles."

—*Byron.*

The rattles of this preeminent child of Murder were heard in deafening clatter over all Europe for twenty years; there is a singular dearth of the acts that have honest fame or that conduce to self-approbation. A steely selfishness from first to last marks the career of Napoleon Bonaparte.

Nearly a hundred years have passed away since Nap's dread Waterloo. There have been wars since then and much blood has flowed, tho' perhaps of no one battle since Waterloo may it decisively be said that had victory gone other than it did go, all subsequent history would be essentially different from what it is.

Perhaps in our Civil War the three days' battle of Gettysburg may seem to hold a determinant place. The continuance of slavery and the break up of the young Republic of the West would surely have made a momentous page of history—but one with which we are happily unfamiliar. Nor would the import of that page affect only us and our Republic; both continents are now more or less favorably influenced by what we now are, so may they have been unfavorably influenced by what we might have been. But Gettysburg is too near for perfect vision. Then, too, the personal element, favorable or unfavorable, is conducive to myopia. So with Waterloo, secure in a hundred years' perspective, the Battles of Destiny end.

In a hasty glance over the historic field from Memphis, 5000 B. C. to Mexico, 1914 A. D.—the great conflicts of nations loom sullenly as blood red peaks daubing the darkness. There is no sequence; they lead nowhere; they just sullenly, luridly bleed. Memphis; Nineveh; Babylon; Marathon, Salamis, Syracuse, Ægospotami, Leuctra, Mantinea, Chæronea; Granicus, Issus, Arbela; Ipsus; Cannæ, Zama, Cynoscephalæ, Magnesia, Pharsalia, Philippi, Actium; Teutobergerwald; Chalons; Tours, Hastings, Orleans; Lepanto; Blenheim; Naseby; Pultova; Saratoga; Valmy; Waterloo; Gettysburg; Mukden; Adrianople; Mexico—as blood red peaks dot the darkness. Is warfare and concomitant hate the natural state of man? The peaks ooze blood in answer.

Some pessimistic glimmerings of the Epicurean philosophy seem to scintillate out from the past. And that philosophy, crystallized in Lucretius' cynic saying, *Homo homini lupus* (One man is a wolf to another man) glitters in icicle harshness and coldness down in the darkness. And yet amidst this general censure of the heart of man I hear a shrill true cry of self exculpation. I am not a wolf to man or beast or bird. My hands are clean; my heart is kind. Am I unique in the human nature plan? No. May I affirm of self that which I deny of others? No. My own light illumines the darkness and leads upward and on.

Cease Firing, Lay Down Your Arms, "We speak for those (dumb animals) who cannot speak for themselves"; "I would not enter on my list of friends the man who needlessly sets foot upon a worm"; "He who is not actively kind is cruel"—are among the utterances of the hour that tip the farthest pendulum-swing from old Lucretius' snarl. Wars must cease. The searchlight of civilization's best thought and feelings is turned full upon war—showing its hitherto darkly concealed causes; its concomitant wrongs, sufferings, shamble horrors; its calamitous, nation-suicidal results. However necessary or inevitable the arbitrament by the sword may have been in the past, it is so no longer.

Let wars cease: in the name of all the bloody battlefields from Marathon to Waterloo; and in pity for all the war-woe from Egypt's Memphis down to Mexico—let wars cease.

Lector House believes that a society develops through a two-fold approach of continuous learning and adaptation, which is derived from the study of classic literary works spread across the historic timeline of literature records. Therefore, we aim at reviving, repairing and redeveloping all those inaccessible or damaged but historically as well as culturally important literature across subjects so that the future generations may have an opportunity to study and learn from past works to embark upon a journey of creating a better future.

This book is a result of an effort made by Lector House towards making a contribution to the preservation and repair of original ancient works which might hold historical significance to the approach of continuous learning across subjects.

HAPPY READING & LEARNING!

LECTOR HOUSE LLP
E-MAIL: lectorpublishing@gmail.com

Lightning Source UK Ltd.
Milton Keynes UK
UKHW010648090820
367908UK00002B/368